RAND NATIONAL DEFENSE RESEARCH INSTITUTE

T0294857

Hispanic Representation in the Department of Defense Civilian Workforce

Trend and Barrier Analysis

Miriam Matthews, Bruce R. Orvis, David Schulker,

Kimberly Curry Hall, Abigail Haddad,

Stefan Matthew Zavislan, Nelson Lim

Prepared for the Office of the Secretary of Defense
Approved for public release; distribution unlimited

For more information on this publication, visit www.rand.org/t/RR1699

Library of Congress Control Number: 2017951391

ISBN: 978-0-8330-9900-6

www.rand.org

Preface

Recent reports published by the U.S. Office of Personnel Management have shown underrepresentation of Hispanics in the federal government in comparison to the U.S. civilian labor force. These reports have also shown that, in comparison to other executive departments in the federal government, the U.S. Department of Defense (DoD) has one of the lowest proportions of Hispanics in its workforce. These reports suggest that Hispanic underrepresentation requires additional consideration in DoD but do not sufficiently consider what might contribute to limited DoD employment of this group.

This report provides information that might assist DoD in addressing Hispanic underrepresentation in its civilian workforce. It describes analyses that agencies have used for assessing barriers to employment in the federal workforce and includes barrier analyses that we conducted to assess Hispanic representation in DoD. It also includes results of an innovative new analytic option to determine whether certain workforce characteristics might influence Hispanic representation, and it includes analyses examining Hispanic representation among USAJOBS applicants to DoD. Further, the report includes information from interviews we conducted to examine practices in place in DoD and other federal agencies for recruitment of Hispanic civilians and information from interviews conducted with hiring managers within DoD that addressed perceptions of Hispanic employment and ideas for promoting the employment of this group. Finally, the report makes recommendations based on these analyses.

The research was sponsored by the Office of Diversity Management and Equal Opportunity in the Office of the Secretary of Defense and conducted within the Forces and Resources Policy Center of the RAND National Defense Research Institute, a federally funded research and development center sponsored by the Office of the Secretary of Defense, the Joint Staff, the Unified Combatant Commands, the Navy, the Marine Corps, the defense agencies, and the defense Intelligence Community.

For more information on the RAND Forces and Resources Policy Center, see www.rand.org/nsrd/ndri/centers/frp or contact the director (contact information is provided on the web page). The appendixes for this report are available at www.rand.org/pubs/research_reports/RR1699.html.

Contents

Figures

Tables

Summary

Hispanics are less represented in the federal government workforce than in the U.S. civilian labor force (CLF) and particularly underrepresented in the civilian workforce of the U.S. Department of Defense (DoD). Although previous analyses have demonstrated that Hispanics are underrepresented in DoD, research has not yet considered employment barriers for Hispanics across DoD agencies. In this report, we provide information that might help DoD address Hispanic underrepresentation in its civilian workforce.[1]

To do so, we review and conduct several analyses, including those that the U.S. Equal Employment Opportunity Commission (EEOC) suggests for assessing barriers to employment in the federal workforce. We examine trends in Hispanic employment in the DoD, non-DoD federal, and civilian workforces, and we consider what factors might account for Hispanic underrepresentation in DoD. We also explore data on job applicants. To conduct these analyses, we utilize data that the U.S. Office of Personnel Management (OPM) maintains on federal employees and on job applicants and applications submitted through USAJOBS and data that the U.S. Census Bureau collects through the American Community Survey (ACS). We also present findings from interviews with representatives of DoD and of Hispanic-serving institutions (HSIs).

Research on Hispanic Employment in the U.S. Civilian Labor Force

Research on Hispanic employment in the United States has considered at least two issues of particular interest for this report: (1) how to measure race and ethnicity and (2) employment among those who identify as Hispanic.

---

[1] Other research suggests that Hispanics are also underrepresented among active-duty military personnel (Asch et al., 2009).

Measuring and Reporting Race and Ethnicity

To assist with reporting and measuring race and ethnicity, the Office of Management and Budget (OMB) identifies five primary racial categories of interest to the federal government:

- American Indian or Alaska native
- Asian
- black or African American
- native Hawaiian or other Pacific Islander
- white.

In addition, OMB identifies two ethnic categories of interest:

- Hispanic or Latino
- not Hispanic or Latino.

Every federal agency must provide information to EEOC regarding the distribution of its workforce by race, ethnicity, and sex. Such categories are based on employee self-identification, but federal agencies will visually identify and designate a race and Hispanic identification for employees where necessary. In this report, we use data conforming to OMB standards whether gathered by self-identification or observer identification of individuals.

Hispanics in the Civilian Labor Force

We provide a brief description of Hispanics in the CLF because this is the population to which Hispanics in DoD are compared. The total CLF, as reported by the Census Bureau and the U.S. Bureau of Labor Statistics, includes people who are at least 16 years of age, reside in the 50 states or the District of Columbia, are not in institutions (e.g., penal facilities, mental facilities), are not on active duty in the armed forces, and are either employed or unemployed but available or looking for work (U.S. Census Bureau, 2010). Notably, the CLF is not limited to U.S. citizens. Hispanics make up 16 percent of the CLF but 20 percent of those in the CLF who are unemployed. In addition, they are less likely to have completed high school than non-Hispanics (based on 2013 Current Population Survey data [U.S. Bureau of Labor Statistics, 2014a]).

Application of Prior Guidance and Analytic Efforts to Hispanic Employment in the Department of Defense

Title VII, Section 717 of the Civil Rights Act of 1964 (Pub. L. 88-352) establishes that U.S. executive agencies and military departments (excluding uniformed members) must annually review their affirmative action programs for equal employment opportunity (EEO) on the basis of race, color, religion, sex, and national origin. Section 717 also establishes that EEOC is responsible for reviewing and approving the affirmative action programs and operations of each federal executive agency and military department. EEOC provides guidance for affirmative action programs and for assessing workforce data.

Prior Guidance and Analytic Efforts Addressing Barrier Analyses

Specifically, EEOC's EEO Management Directive (MD) 715 communicates affirmative action program standards to federal agencies and establishes reporting requirements for these entities. EEO MD-715 instructs federal executive agencies and military departments (excluding uniformed personnel) to review their workforce characteristics annually in order to assess whether there might be barriers to the employment of certain groups, including Hispanics, in the agencies' workforces. To determine whether federal agencies and military departments (excluding uniformed personnel) have adequate representation and participation of Hispanics in different grades, occupations, and other workforce classifications, EEOC requires agencies to compare their rates with those in a benchmark population. For racial and ethnic groups, the rates for this benchmark population come from the relevant CLF.[2]

Evaluation of Workforce Data

If agencies find lower rates of representation and participation for Hispanics than are evident in the CLF (EEOC, 2004), barriers to Hispanic employment might exist. If agencies find discrepancies indicating possible employment barriers, EEOC requires that they conduct more in-depth assessments into the potential causes for these discrepancies (EEOC, 2014). For example, if a group's representation within an agency is 0.5 percent less than that group's representation in the CLF, a discrepancy might be present. Determination of whether a representation discrepancy is sufficiently large to trigger further analyses depends, in part, on an EEOC reviewer's discretion (EEOC, 2014).

Different federal agencies have different workforce structures, sizes, locations, occupations, and other characteristics, so it can be challenging to standardize an approach or a set of approaches that is appropriate to use in assessing the magnitude of representation discrepancies across all agencies and all groups. Therefore, EEOC does not provide a standard rule of thumb or guideline for all agencies to use to evaluate the severity, or magnitude, of discrepancies between agency and CLF group representations. The lack of a standard rule of thumb or complementary set of rules of thumb can contribute to confusion among agencies when evaluating the magnitude of their own representation discrepancies with the CLF, and the absence of a standard rule

---

[2] For federal agencies, EEO MD-715 tables use only those who are U.S. citizens. For private entities, they include both those who are and those who are not U.S. citizens. Online Appendix B reproduces samples of these tables.

of thumb or set of rules of thumb might lead different reviewers to come to different conclusions regarding the presence of employment barriers when evaluating the same workforce data. It was outside the scope of the current project to collect and evaluate all potential rules of thumb that could be used for evaluating the magnitude of a representation discrepancy. A working group of practitioners, social and behavioral scientists, and representatives from federal agencies might be able to establish more-definitive rules of thumb for federal agencies to use when evaluating representation discrepancies, which might provide agencies with much-needed guidance in this area.

Assessment of Discrepancies

In this report, we describe possible rules of thumb that agencies might use to determine the presence of discrepancies or representation triggers. None of the rules of thumb we describe is without fault, and there is no universally accepted assessment or combination of assessments for identifying the presence of large discrepancies in employment rates. Although we review and consider these rules, we do not endorse them as stand-alone evidence of the presence of employment barriers. Rather, readers and practitioners should interpret these rules of thumb as data points in an analysis, not as final determinations of the presence or absence of employment barriers.

One of these rules of thumb involves addressing any observed discrepancies between the proportion of a given group in a workforce and the proportion of that group in the CLF. Another rule of thumb is an 80-percent, or four-fifths, rule. Under this rule, a selection rate for one racial or ethnic group that is less than 80 percent of that for another group would indicate a possible barrier. A third rule of thumb identifies workforce proportions that are at least two standard deviations from that of an observed reference group.

The 80-percent rule of thumb and two–standard deviation rule of thumb are often used to assess adverse or disparate impact. Adverse or disparate impact occurs when an employment practice (e.g., selection or promotion) has a disadvantageous effect on members of a protected group, regardless of whether this effect was intended.[3] These rules are less frequently used to compare the representation of a group within an agency (e.g., DoD) to the representation of that group in a larger labor force (e.g., CLF). In the absence of legislated or widely used rules of thumb that explicitly provide guidance regarding comparisons between an agency's group representation and that group's representation in a larger labor force, we draw from these available rules of thumb as examples for comparisons between DoD and the larger CLF. However, we acknowledge that application of these rules of thumb to this particular context is not ideal. We also acknowledge that various other rules from the adverse-impact analysis literature could be considered in this context or that new rules could be developed for use in this context.

---

[3] EEOC uniform guidelines (Title 29 of the Code of Federal Regulations [CFR], Part 1507) outline rules of thumb that can be used to determine whether adverse impact is present.

Other Common Triggers

Discrepancies between agency and standard CLF rates of participation and representation are triggers for more in-depth assessments to identify employment barriers and to address whether an agency's EEO program has deficiencies (EEOC, 2014). Lower representation of Hispanics in the agency workforce than in the relevant CLF is one potential trigger. Others include

- *low entry–high exit*, caused by a group with a low rate of participation in a workforce having a low rate of entry to but high rate of exit from that workforce
- *glass wall*, indicated by a group's low levels of representation in occupations that are tracked for upward mobility
- *blocked pipeline*, indicated by a group's low rate of promotion within certain occupations
- *glass ceiling*, indicated by a group's low rate of participation in and promotion into leadership positions.

Application to Department of Defense Hispanic Employment Barrier Analyses

To identify possible barriers to Hispanic employment in DoD, we conducted barrier analyses that compared the proportion of Hispanics among full-time, nonseasonal permanent civilian employees within DoD and its components (i.e., Air Force, Army, Navy, and Fourth Estate) to the rest of the federal workforce and the CLF.[4]

Overall Hispanic Representation in the Federal Workforce, Department of Defense Civilian Workforce, and Civilian Labor Force

DoD has a lower percentage of Hispanics among its employees than both the non-DoD federal civilian workforce and the CLF. In 2013, 6.5 percent of DoD employees were Hispanic citizens, compared with 9.3 percent among other federal civilian workers and 11.4 percent of the CLF. Hispanic representation in the CLF and the non-DoD federal civilian workforce increased more rapidly from 2008 to 2013 than it did in DoD. The rules of thumb identified above show that the discrepancy between Hispanic participation in DoD and that elsewhere might be indicative of possible employment barriers.

---

[4] The Fourth Estate in this context includes the following agencies: Defense Acquisition University, Defense Advanced Research Projects Agency, Defense Commissary Agency, Defense Contract Audit Agency, Defense Contract Management Agency, Defense Finance and Accounting Service, Defense Health Agency, Defense Human Resource Activity, Defense Information Systems Agency, Defense Legal Services Agency, Defense Logistics Agency, Defense Media Activity, Defense Microelectronics Activity, Defense POW [Prisoner of War]/ MIA [Missing in Action] Accounting Agency, Defense Security Cooperation Agency, Defense Security Service, Defense Technical Information Center, Defense Technology Security Administration, Defense Threat Reduction Agency, DoD Education Activity, DoD Office of Inspector General, Joint Staff, Missile Defense Agency, National Defense University, Office of Economic Adjustment, Office of the Secretary of Defense, Pentagon Force Protection Agency, U.S. Court of Appeals for the Armed Forces, and Washington Headquarters Services. The Marine Corps is a component of the Navy.

DoD components (i.e., Air Force, Army, Navy, and Fourth Estate) vary in their employment of Hispanics. In 2013, the Department of the Army had the highest proportion of Hispanics among civilian workers, 7.4 percent, while the Fourth Estate had the lowest, 5.2 percent.

Other Common Triggers

Several common triggers also indicate possible Hispanic employment barriers. Hispanics comprised 5.2 percent of new hires but 6.0 percent of exits in the DoD workforce from 2008 to 2013. They were more concentrated in occupations with lower rates of promotion and less likely to be promoted in occupations with higher rates of promotion. Hispanics comprised 8.0 percent of the DoD civilian workforce in General Schedule lower grades, 6.0 percent of that in middle grades, and 4.5 percent of that in upper grades.

Analyzing Differences in Hispanic Representation Across Labor Forces

To determine the extent to which observable differences (such as differences between the types of jobs available, education requirements, and job locations) can explain Hispanic underrepresentation in the DoD civilian workforce, we conducted two types of analyses. First, we compared the characteristics of the DoD, non-DoD federal, and CLF workforces. Second, we sought to determine statistically how much of the Hispanic underrepresentation can be attributed to observable differences and how much is attributable to unobserved differences requiring further exploration. Unlike the previously described assessments of discrepancies, we kept noncitizens in these analyses because that allowed us to examine the impact that the government policy of employing only citizens has on Hispanic representation in DoD.

Characteristics of Each Workforce

Table S.1 summarizes characteristics of the civilian workforces in DoD agencies, the CLF, and the non-DoD federal workforce for the data used in this portion of the analysis. As earlier indicated, the DoD civilian workforce is much less Hispanic than other federal agencies or the CLF. DoD civilian workers differ from both the CLF and the non-DoD federal workforce in other dimensions, such as age, veteran status, and the types of occupations that they perform.

Blinder–Oaxaca Decomposition

One way to think of the relationship between each workforce's characteristics and the Hispanic representation gap is to ask the following question: If the DoD workforce had the same characteristics as others (e.g., the CLF or non-DoD federal workforce) on factors other than race and ethnicity, how much would the gap narrow? If adjusting for these characteristics narrows the gap, we can conclude that at least some of the gap is

Table S.1
Individual and Occupation Characteristics in the Three Workforces

Variable	DoD Agencies (1)	CLF (2)	Non-DoD Federal Workforce (3)
Race/ethnic group, as a percentage			
White	69.7	66.3	62.1
Black or African American	15.8	10.5	19.8
Hispanic or Latino	6.3	15.6	9.3
Asian, native Hawaiian, or other Pacific Islander	6.0	5.7	5.7
Other	2.2	2.0	3.1
Female, as a percentage	34.1	43.1	48.6
Employee age, in years	47.5	43.1	46.8
Educational attainment, in years	14.6	13.8	15.0
U.S. citizen, as a percentage	100.0	91.3	99.9
Veteran, as a percentage	45.9	5.8	21.9
Occupational category, as a percentage			
Professional, white collar	25.1	19.3	27.0
Administrative, white collar	36.6	16.4	41.1
Technical, white collar	14.5	9.6	18.1
Clerical, white collar	3.9	18.3	5.3
Other, white collar	3.4	5.3	4.4
Blue collar	16.6	31.1	4.2
Resides in a metropolitan area, as a percentage	97.9	96.1	96.7
Federal job category, as a percentage			
Competitive service	93.0		69.3
Excepted service	6.8		30.1
Senior Executive Service general	0.1		0.3
Senior Executive Service career reserved	0.1		0.3
N	611,693	925,468	1,148,495

SOURCES: 2013 OPM data for DoD and 2013 ACS data for the CLF.

NOTE: For each variable in the table, all of the differences between columns (1) and (2) and between columns (1) and (3) are statistically significant at the $\alpha = 0.01$ level. The numbers in this table differ slightly from those presented earlier because we included a different set of observations in the data. This analysis included noncitizens in the CLF to examine the impact of citizenship and excluded part-time workers and federal employees. This analysis also excluded personnel in the OPM data who had missing information in one or more of the necessary variables.

related to the workforce characteristics. If the gap remains or increases after accounting for the characteristics, the conclusion would be that other factors are driving the Hispanic underrepresentation in DoD.

Figure S.1 indicates that nearly the entire gap is attributable to workforce characteristics. The first column of the figure shows Hispanic presence in the CLF, 15.6 percent. The second column shows Hispanic presence in the DoD civilian workforce, 6.3 percent, and the representation gap of 9.3 percentage points. The third column displays the results of the decomposition analysis. It shows that approximately 2 percentage points of the gap are attributable to educational differences. That is, if the educational characteristics of the DoD civilian workforce were the same as those of the CLF, the gap in Hispanic representation would be closer to 7 than 9 percent. Other substantial contributors to Hispanic underrepresentation in the DoD workforce are citizenship, veteran's status, age, location, and occupation. The fourth column depicts the gap that remains after accounting for workforce characteristics, i.e., the unexplained portion of the gap. That is, it shows that a gap of 0.7 percentage points would remain even if DoD civilian workers were identical in the average observable characteristics listed with all CLF workers.

Figure S.1
Difference in Hispanic Representation Between the Department of Defense Workforce and the Civilian Labor Force, with Decomposition Results

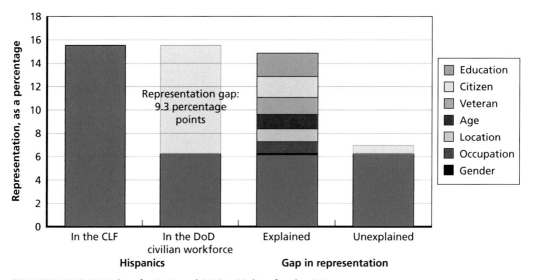

SOURCES: 2013 OPM data for DoD and 2013 ACS data for the CLF.
RAND RR1699-S.1

Job-Applicant Data and Hispanic Representation in the Department of Defense Civilian Workforce

To identify current prospects for bringing more Hispanics into the DoD civilian work-force, we examined characteristics of people who apply for DoD jobs and engage in the federal hiring process. We used data on DoD job applicants captured through the federal government's official online job listing site, USAJOBS.gov, and compared it to information on the DoD civilian workforce gleaned from data that OPM provided.

Hispanic Representation Through the Department of Defense Application Process

Most job applicants do not provide their ethnicity on USAJOBS, so we could not determine whether or not they are Hispanic. Given such missing data, we calculated a plausible range of values for representation at each phase of the process. Specifically, we calculated Hispanic representation under an upper-bound assumption that Hispanic and non-Hispanic applicants are equally likely to provide ethnicity information and a lower-bound assumption that all missing ethnicity information is from non-Hispanics. Our analyses suggested that the true representation level of Hispanics for DoD is prob-ably closer to the lower-bound assumption. Regardless of the assumption, it is evident that Hispanic representation decreases as the process progresses from application to hire, as Figure S.2 illustrates.

Department of Defense Job Characteristics That Increase the Likelihood of an Applicant Being Hispanic

We identified several characteristics of jobs that might affect the likelihood of a His-panic applicant, and subsequent hire, for a job. Among DoD jobs offered in 2014, job location has perhaps the greatest effect. For example, DoD jobs in New Mexico were 15 percentage points more likely to receive a Hispanic applicant than jobs elsewhere. There is also some evidence that Hispanic DoD applicants might be more interested in work requiring less education or experience—perhaps this is because Hispanics in the CLF, on average, are younger and less educated than non-Hispanics. Similarly, jobs at higher pay grades were less likely to receive Hispanic applicants.

Interview Findings on Hispanic Representation Gaps in the Department of Defense Civilian Workforce

To complement our quantitative analyses and gain additional insight on Hispanic underrepresentation in the DoD civilian workforce, we conducted qualitative analyses involving interviews of DoD representatives, HSI representatives, and others.[5] Among

---

[5] We received approval from the RAND Human Subjects Protection Committee for all components of this research report, including interviews. DoD's Research Regulatory Oversight Office also reviewed and concurred

Figure S.2
**Hispanic Representation, by Application Stage, with Civilian Labor Force and Department of
Defense Employee Benchmarks: 2013 and 2014**

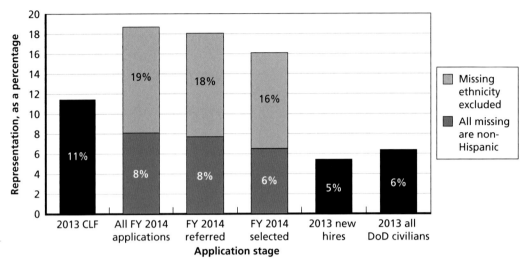

SOURCES: 2013 OPM data for DoD and 2013 ACS data for the CLF.
NOTE: FY = fiscal year.
RAND RR1699-S.2

DoD interviewees, the most–frequently mentioned potential barriers to Hispanic
employment were geographic location of positions, perceptions of language or citizenship barriers, and a lack of awareness and motivation from leaders and managers to
address Hispanic underrepresentation. DoD interviewees noted varying levels of effort
related to Hispanic outreach in their organizations and suggested more partnerships
with professional Hispanic groups and recruitment at HSIs and in areas with high
Hispanic populations as means of reducing Hispanic underrepresentation. Many interviewees did not report hiring strategies specifically targeted at Hispanics.

DoD interviewees noted challenges with the USAJOBS process and perceived
the process as cumbersome and time-consuming. They said that Hispanic applicants
might be deterred from applying or lose patience with the system, making it difficult
for DoD to compete with the private sector for them. Although interviewees stated that
few strategies exist to promote and retain Hispanic employees, many noted that mentoring programs and Hispanic employee resource groups (ERGs) helped communicate
career-development opportunities and build a community for Hispanic employees.

with the RAND Human Subjects Protection Committee's approval for this research.

Interview Findings on Department of Defense Recruitment at Hispanic-Serving Institutions

Our interviews with HSI representatives included representatives from the Hispanic Association of Colleges and Universities; California State University, Los Angeles; California State University, San Bernardino; Colorado State University–Pueblo; Florida International University; New Jersey City University; University of New Mexico; University of Texas at El Paso; University of Texas at San Antonio; Palo Alto College (community); and Valencia College (community). HSI representatives perceived that there were several effective strategies to connect students with employment opportunities. Among these strategies were active on-campus marketing by organizations beyond attending job fairs or similar events, connecting with relevant student organizations on campus, and involving alumni in recruiting efforts. Interviewees also stressed the importance of early engagement, including outreach to students early in their college careers through internships.

HSI representatives also noted that DoD engagement with their students was limited. Like DoD interviewees, HSI representatives stated that students find the USAJOBS process complex and time-consuming. They recommended that DoD engage with promising candidates throughout the application process. Interviewees also noted a lack of awareness of DoD civilian opportunities among students and suggested that DoD communicate job opportunities and career paths in ways more interesting and appealing to youth. HSI representatives said that students might hesitate to relocate to new areas and suggested that DoD connect with students' families when possible, as well as work to build networks for new employees once relocated.

Conclusion and Recommendations

Our findings suggest several potential options that DoD might pursue in assessing and improving Hispanic representation in the DoD civilian workforce. These include better marketing of DoD opportunities, better means of engaging and understand potential Hispanic workers, and better means to support Hispanic workers DoD does hire.

Expand Department of Defense Outreach to the Hispanic Population, Especially to Younger Hispanic Workers in U.S. Hispanic Population Centers

The Hispanic representation gap in DoD might not improve without proactive efforts to increase Hispanic awareness of work for DoD. One effort DoD can make is to expand outreach efforts to Hispanic workers. DoD efforts should focus most heavily on younger potential workers, among whom, our analyses show, its underrepresentation problem is worst. DoD has an advantage in attracting Hispanics to jobs in states where it has a substantial presence and the Hispanic population percentage is high.

Increase Department of Defense Presence with Hispanic Student Populations at Colleges and Universities, Particularly Hispanic-Serving Institutions

In addition to expanding outreach to large Hispanic population centers, DoD should increase its presence among Hispanic student populations at colleges and universities, particularly at HSIs. This will help increase awareness of DoD civilian opportunities and application processes and allow face-to-face interactions with potential applicants. Such efforts might also allow DoD to inform students' families of what DoD careers offer and to assuage concerns about potential moves to new areas of the country. Where possible, DoD should involve DoD employees who are HSI alumni in campus recruiting efforts.

Stay Engaged with Promising Candidates During the Application Process, and, When Possible, Leverage Appropriate Hiring Authorities

Hispanic candidates can face barriers in the application and hiring process. Perceptions that USAJOBS.gov is complex and time-consuming might pose one barrier. To combat this potential barrier, DoD should encourage recruiters, hiring managers, and other relevant personnel to follow up with promising candidates during the process and encourage them to stay engaged with DoD.

Support the Development of Hispanic-Friendly Communities in the Workplace Through Employee Resource Groups and Mentoring

To improve promotion opportunities for Hispanic employees and retain more of them, DoD should support the development of Hispanic-friendly communities, such as ERGs, at work. By fostering an inclusive environment that is welcoming to Hispanics, DoD can help Hispanic workers flourish in their jobs and desire to stay in DoD careers. To be effective and have credibility, DoD should ensure that ERGs have senior-level support and endorsement. DoD can also foster an inclusive environment and support for Hispanic employees through mentoring. DoD should increase the emphasis on mentoring Hispanic employees throughout the department. It could do so by leveraging existing mentoring programs available to all employees.

Improve the Accessibility, Accuracy, and Utility of Job-Applicant Data

Our analyses demonstrated the potential usefulness of job-applicant data but also found some limitations in how DoD collects and uses applicant data. The limited information available could lead to erroneous conclusions if the nuances of data collection are not transparent. This suggests that analytic errors involving data obtained from USAJOBS can occur over time or across different data analysts. DoD should review the process of collecting data from USAJOBS so as to improve the accuracy of applicant information.

Conclusion

Our analyses suggest several contributors to Hispanic underrepresentation in the DoD civilian workforce and throughout the employment cycle. Our recommendations address each phase of the employment cycle, from outreach to retention. By implementing the initiatives we recommend, DoD can progress toward overcoming potential barriers to Hispanic representation in its civilian workforce. To determine whether implementation of these initiatives has an impact on Hispanic employment, DoD will need to conduct corresponding evaluations.

Acknowledgments

We wish to thank Clarence Johnson, director of the Office of Diversity Management and Equal Opportunity (ODMEO); Beatrice Bernfeld, director of equal employment opportunity in ODMEO; and F. Michael Sena, deputy director of ODMEO for their thoughtful input on this project. We would also like to thank the hiring managers and supervisors throughout the federal civilian workforce, and the U.S. Department of Defense in particular, who provided information to us and participated in discussions with us. In addition, we thank the Defense Civilian Personnel Advisory Service for its assistance with applicant flow data. We also thank the Hispanic Association of Colleges and Universities and those at the various Hispanic-serving institutions who spoke with us. We thank the Equal Employment Opportunity Commission and the Office of Personnel Management for providing information and helpful responses to our multiple inquiries. We thank Michael Ryan Vasseur and Shamena Anwar for their assistance with analyses, and we thank John D. Winkler, Lisa M. Harrington, Craig Bond, and Sarah O. Meadows for their feedback throughout this project. We thank Beth J. Asch for her comments on earlier analyses conducted as part of this research, and we thank Kirsten M. Keller and Veronica Venture for their thorough review and helpful comments on drafts of this report. We also thank Clifford A. Grammich, who provided editorial assistance.

Abbreviations

ACS	American Community Survey
AFD	applicant flow data
CBSA	Core Based Statistical Area
CFR	Code of Federal Regulations
CLF	civilian labor force
DCMA	Defense Contract Management Agency
DCPAS	Defense Civilian Personnel Advisory Service
DFAS	Defense Finance and Accounting Service
D&I	diversity and inclusion
DIR	Diplomat in Residence
DLA	Defense Logistics Agency
DoD	U.S. Department of Defense
DoDD	Department of Defense directive
EEO	equal employment opportunity
EEOC	U.S. Equal Employment Opportunity Commission
EO	executive order
ERG	employee resource group
FEORP	Federal Equal Opportunity Recruitment Program
FY	fiscal year
GS	General Schedule
HACU	Hispanic Association of Colleges and Universities
HBCU	historically black college or university

HCFE	Hispanic Council on Federal Employment
HEAT	Hispanic Engagement Action Team
HEPM	Hispanic Employment Program Manager
HNIP	Hispanic Association of Colleges and Universities National Internship Program
HSI	Hispanic-serving institution
IPA	Intergovernmental Personnel Act
MCO	mission-critical occupation
MD	management directive
NAVAIR	U.S. Navy Naval Air Systems Command
OCONUS	outside the continental United States
ODMEO	Office of Diversity Management and Equal Opportunity
OMB	Office of Management and Budget
OPM	U.S. Office of Personnel Management
OSD	Office of the Secretary of Defense
PATCOB	professional, white collar; administrative, white collar; technical, white collar; clerical, white collar; other, white collar; and blue collar
PMC	President's Management Council
RAD	Recruitment Assistance Division
SEP	Special Emphasis Program
SES	Senior Executive Service
SHPE	Society of Hispanic Professional Engineers
STAR	Student Training and Academic Recruitment
STEM	science, technology, engineering, and math
USD(AT&L)	Under Secretary of Defense for Acquisition, Technology and Logistics
USD Comptroller	Under Secretary of Defense Comptroller
USD(P&R)	Under Secretary of Defense for Personnel and Readiness

CHAPTER ONE

Introduction

The numbers and proportions of Hispanics in the United States are increasing (Ennis, Ríos-Vargas, and Albert, 2011). As their population increases, their proportion in the total U.S. civilian labor force (CLF), which includes the number of Americans who are seeking or have jobs and are not institutionalized or serving in the military, is also expected to increase (Toossi, 2013). The federal government—notably, the U.S. Department of Defense (DoD)—must make proactive efforts to promote Hispanic representation within its workforce that matches its current and growing representation in the comparable CLF.[1]

Thus far, the federal government and DoD have made multiple efforts to promote Hispanic representation. For example, several executive orders (EOs) address Hispanic representation in the federal workforce, including EO 13171, "Hispanic Employment in the Federal Government"; EO 13562, "Recruiting and Hiring Students and Recent Graduates"; and EO 13583, "Establishing a Coordinated Government-Wide Initiative to Promote Diversity and Inclusion in the Federal Workforce." In addition, the U.S. Office of Personnel Management (OPM), which is charged with ensuring successful federal workforce management, has released strategic plans addressing Hispanic representation in the federal workforce and has established the Hispanic Council on Federal Employment (HCFE). The U.S. Equal Employment Opportunity Commission (EEOC) has also established the federal Hispanic Work Group to develop strategies for improving Hispanic employment issues. Further, several efforts within DoD might address Hispanic underrepresentation in the DoD workforce, including the 2014 Human Goals Charter (DoD, 2014b) that affirms the department's commitment to diversity and inclusion (D&I) (for more information on relevant legal requirements and initiatives, see online Appendix A).

Despite these efforts, OPM reports (OPM, undated [b]; OPM, 2016) have shown that Hispanics are underrepresented in the federal government civilian workforce, particularly in the civilian workforce of DoD. However, research has not yet identified what contributes to Hispanic representation across the DoD civilian workforce. To

---

[1] The comparable CLF for the federal government typically includes only those in the CLF who are U.S. citizens, excluding those who are not U.S. citizens.

better understand Hispanic underrepresentation in this workforce and how to address it, the Office of the Secretary of Defense (OSD) Office of Diversity Management and Equal Opportunity (ODMEO) asked RAND to examine contributors to underrepresentation of Hispanic civilians in DoD and provide recommendations for DoD employment policies and practices based on these analyses.

Approach

Our work encompassed multiple elements. We reviewed guidance that EEOC provides for barrier analyses that federal government agencies conduct. We then conducted analyses examining characteristics of DoD-employed civilians. To do so, we analyzed OPM data on civilian employees across the federal government and data from the American Community Survey (ACS), a nationwide annual survey that complements the decennial census, on the CLF. After that, we used these same data to explore whether DoD labor-force characteristics might account for Hispanic underrepresentation in DoD.

In addition to assessing DoD civilian employee data, we considered trends among applicants and applications to DoD civilian positions. To do so, we analyzed DoD applicant and application data from 2012 to 2014 from USAJOBS.gov, linking this information to corresponding job announcements. We also analyzed USA Staffing applicant flow data (AFD) for fiscal year (FY) 2014. USA Staffing is an automated hiring software system that OPM provides to federal agencies.

Further, we complemented these quantitative analyses with qualitative assessments. To do so, we interviewed representatives of Hispanic-serving institutions (HSIs), DoD and its components, and other federal agencies. In these interviews, we addressed possible barriers to Hispanic employment and strategies that have been or could be used to address these barriers.[2]

Organization of This Report

The remaining chapters in this report provide additional information, our analyses, and our recommendations. Chapter Two reviews trends in Hispanic representation in the CLF. Chapter Three describes previous guidance and analyses for assessing barriers to employment in the federal workforce, and it describes our analyses of trends in Hispanic workforce representation in DoD, other federal agencies, and the CLF. Chapter Four explores whether DoD labor-force characteristics might account for Hispanic

---

[2] We received approval from the RAND Human Subjects Protection Committee for all components of this research report, including interviews. DoD's Research Regulatory Oversight Office also reviewed and concurred with the RAND Human Subjects Protection Committee's approval for this research.

underrepresentation in DoD. Chapter Five examines observed trends in applicants and applications to DoD, drawing from quantitative data available from OPM, USA-JOBS, and the ACS. Chapter Six presents information we obtained in interviews with DoD hiring managers and supervisors, and Chapter Seven describes information we obtained in interviews with representatives of HSIs and other non-DoD federal agencies. Chapter Eight provides several avenues by which DoD might promote Hispanic representation in its workforce.

Several appendixes (available online) complement our research. Appendix A describes legal requirements and initiatives regarding employment of Hispanics. Appendix B provides example workforce data tables that EEOC has used. Appendix C describes additional analyses that we conducted to complement the analyses in Chapter Three. Appendix D provides information for several different occupations for DoD and its components. Appendix E provides additional information regarding quantitative analyses we conducted. Appendix F lists the questions we used in our DoD interviews, and Appendix G lists them for our HSI interviews.

CHAPTER TWO

Research on Hispanic Employment in the U.S. Civilian Labor Force

To describe the characteristics of all Hispanics in the United States, as well as those in the CLF—the population of interest in the EEOC barrier analyses that federal agencies conduct (EEOC, 2004)—we undertake two tasks in this chapter. First, we briefly discuss how researchers and organizations conceptualize race and ethnicity and review past and current standards for the measurement of these concepts and issues that arise with these measurement standards. Second, we provide descriptive information on Hispanics in the CLF.

Race and Ethnicity

A great deal of confusion and debate exist regarding how to define and measure the concepts of race and ethnicity (Omi and Winant, 1994). Different definitions and measurements of these concepts can influence observed representation levels within populations. Commonly held definitions of these concepts can change over time and place (Banks and Eberhardt, 1998; Borstelmann, 2001). Some have suggested a biological component to race and different racial categories (Rushton, 2000). Many social scientists, however, do not believe that racial categories have a biological basis (Cokley and Awad, 2008; Smedley and Smedley, 2005). Rather, they consider race and ethnicity to be social constructs (e.g., Banks and Eberhardt, 1998), such that there are often social consequences to being associated with particular racial or ethnic groups (Cokley and Awad, 2008).

Generally, race and ethnicity can be considered to address different, but overlapping, concepts. Race is often used to address variation in skin color and physical features, which can overlap with some variations in ancestry and geographic location (R. Carter, 1995). Title VII of the Civil Rights Act of 1964 prohibits discrimination based on race, color, national origin, sex, or religion but does not define these concepts. EEOC, 2008b, interprets race as involving variations in skin color, hair texture, or facial features and color as involving variations in complexion, skin pigmentation, skin shade, or skin tone.

Social scientists often conceptualize ethnicity as encompassing cultural character-istics, such that the concept of culture involves shared and learned systems of meanings (Betancourt and López, 1993; Cokley and Awad, 2008). Researchers have also suggested that ethnic groups can be characterized by different nationalities, religious affili-ations, languages, traditions, customs, and rituals (Cokley and Awad, 2008). EEOC, 2008a, suggests that national-origin groups are synonymous with ethnic groups: "A 'national origin group,' often referred to as an 'ethnic group,' is a group of people shar-ing a common language, culture, ancestry, and/or other similar social characteristics." Conceptualizations of race and ethnicity affect measurement and subsequent actions based on measurement.

Measuring and Reporting Race and Ethnicity

In part due to the lack of clarity regarding the concepts of race and ethnicity, there is much debate over how to collect and report information on individual race and eth-nicity in the United States. In 1997, the Office of Management and Budget (OMB) issued Statistical Directive 15 (OMB, 1997b), which mandated five racial and ethnic categories for the U.S. census and U.S. federal agencies (Nobles, 2000):

- American Indian or Alaskan native
- Asian or Pacific Islander
- black
- Hispanic
- white.

Over the next two decades, multiple issues regarding these racial categories were raised, including lack of a response option for multiracial groups, inappropriate or overly limited terminology for the groups listed, and inclusion of Hispanic as a racial designation (OMB, 1994). These concerns stimulated revisions to the statistical direc-tive, which were implemented in October 1997. These revisions list five primary racial categories of interest to the federal government, specifically these (OMB, 1997a):

- American Indian or Alaska native
- Asian
- black or African American
- native Hawaiian or other Pacific Islander
- white.

These revisions also list two ethnic categories of interest:

- Hispanic or Latino
- not Hispanic or Latino.

OMB research does not express a consensus on whether these categories should be assessed through use of one or two questions: "Some who favored asking race/Hispanic origin as one question said many Hispanics do not identify themselves as a race" (OMB, 1995). Nevertheless, OMB, 1995, added, others favored the two-question approach and perceived that "Hispanics were a multiracial population and a cultural (not a race) group" (OMB, 1995).

In asking people to self-identify their race and ethnicity, OMB now indicates that the census and federal agencies should use a two-question format, involving one question on race and one question on ethnicity (OMB, 1997a). If the people of interest do not self-identify, observers can use a combined, one-question format with the following six categories: American Indian or Alaska native, Asian, black or African American, Hispanic or Latino, native Hawaiian or other Pacific Islander, and white. Whether using a two- or one-question format, more than one race can be selected. OMB encourages agencies and organizations to collect greater detail of information on race and ethnicity, but any additional racial or ethnic categories must be amenable to aggregation into the minimum categories for race and ethnicity that OMB provided in 1997.

Measuring and Reporting Race and Ethnicity in the Federal Agencies

Measurement and reporting of race and ethnicity must be considered when managing federal personnel files. Every federal agency must provide information to EEOC regarding the distribution of its workforce by race, ethnicity, and sex.[1] This requires identifying the race and ethnicity of every employee, which agencies should try to obtain through employee self-identification. Following OMB standards, if employees in federal agencies refuse to self-identify, these agencies are instructed to use visual inspection to assign a race and ethnicity to each employee (EEOC, 2008c).

To determine the racial and ethnic categories that agencies should use for reporting, EEOC follows the standards that OMB, 1997a, outlines. EEOC encourages federal agencies to use preformatted workforce data tables that the commission provides (Figure 2.1 illustrates the structure, and online Appendix B provides the populated tables). In these tables, if an employee is Hispanic or Latino, regardless of the race or races with which the employee is associated, that employee is listed only as Hispanic or Latino. If an employee is not Hispanic or Latino, information on the employee's race

---

[1] In federal agencies, including DoD, employers must provide information outlined in Equal Employment Opportunity (EEO) Management Directive (MD) 715.

Figure 2.1
Race and Ethnicity Workforce Data Table Example

Table A1: Total workforce B Distribution by race/ethnicity and sex

Employment tenure	Total employees	Hispanic or Latino		Non-Hispanic or Latino											
				White		Black or African American		Asian		Native Hawaiian or other Pacific Islander		American Indian or Alaska native		Two or more races	
	All	Male	Female	Male	Female	Male	Female	Male	Female	Male	Female	Male	Female	Male	Female

SOURCE: EEOC, undated.

RAND *RR1699-2.1*

or races is provided.[2] Reporting by OPM, which maintains data on civilian employees in the federal workforce, often mirrors this structure (e.g., OPM, undated [b]).

Race and Ethnicity in This Report

Nobles, 2000, notes that "there is no guarantee between the category (or categories) that an individual self-selects and the category under which the individual is officially counted" (p. 164). This highlights the social context of racial and ethnic identification. It also suggests that there is no single, correct way to measure or report race and ethnicity that will fully capture the multiple identities that exist in the United States. In this work, we use data collected under the OMB standards, which might involve self-identification or observer identification of people having Hispanic ethnicity. We do this to address current standards for measuring and reporting in federal agencies, including DoD. Thus, in our data analyses in this report, we use ACS data to assess characteristics of the U.S. population and OPM data when we conduct analyses involving characteristics of the federal workforce. In this report, we count individuals as Hispanic regardless of their identification with a racial category. People who do not identify as Hispanic are counted with their races. However, as suggested from the earlier discussion in this chapter regarding race and ethnicity, use of different standards can be associated with variation in observed representation trends.

Hispanics in the U.S. Civilian Labor Force

Many of the analyses in this report involve comparing Hispanic representation in the DoD workforce with Hispanic representation in the CLF, and our analyses address characteristics of Hispanics in DoD and Hispanics in the CLF. Because the report

---

2   OMB, 1997, has noted that the term *nonwhite* is not to be used in presentation of data on race and ethnicity.

involves extensive comparisons to Hispanics in the CLF, we provide background information regarding this group, focusing on information reported by the Bureau of Labor Statistics. This provides context regarding the population with which federal agencies are to compare their workforces and with which we compare the DoD workforce in this report.

The CLF, as reported by the Census Bureau and the Bureau of Labor Statistics, includes people who

- are 16 years of age and older
- reside in the 50 states or the District of Columbia
- are not in institutions (e.g., penal facilities or mental facilities)
- are not on active duty in the armed forces
- are either employed or unemployed but looking for and available to work (U.S. Census Bureau, 2010).

The CLF is not limited to U.S. citizens. EEOC instructs federal agencies to use data on CLF characteristics to make comparisons with their civilian employees (EEOC, 2004). For example, EEOC instructs federal agencies to compare the proportional representations of racial and ethnic groups in their civilian workforce with the representation of these groups in the CLF to determine whether certain groups, such as Hispanics, are underrepresented. Certain agencies can restrict their comparisons to those in the CLF who are citizens. Whether one compares with all persons in the CLF or only citizens in the CLF does have some implications for analyses of the Hispanic workforce in federal agencies, as addressed later in this report.

Hispanics make up approximately 16 percent of the total CLF; as their population increases, their proportion in the CLF is also expected to increase (Toossi, 2013). By 2022, 19 percent of the total CLF is projected to be Hispanic. Currently, among all Hispanics of working age, 66 percent are in the CLF (U.S. Bureau of Labor Statistics, 2014a). Hispanics are slightly more likely to participate in the labor force than workers in other groups, including Asians (65 percent), whites (64 percent), and blacks (61 percent), while foreign-born Hispanics are more likely to participate in the CLF (70 percent) than native-born ones (63 percent) (U.S. Bureau of Labor Statistics, 2014a).

Notably, job location can influence workforce characteristics, such that workforces in certain locations might have greater Hispanic representation. At the state level, New Mexico has the highest proportion of Hispanics in its labor force (44 percent), followed by Texas (38 percent), California (36 percent), Arizona (31 percent), Nevada (26 percent), and Florida (23 percent) (U.S. Bureau of Labor Statistics, 2014b). The states with the largest numbers of Hispanics in their labor forces are California (6,786,000), Texas (4,934,000), Florida (2,156,000), New York (1,546,000), and Illinois (945,000) (U.S. Bureau of Labor Statistics, 2014b).

As noted above, both those who are employed and those who are not employed but looking or available to work are in the CLF. The overall CLF unemployment rate in 2013 was 7 percent, but that rate for Hispanics was 9 percent (U.S. Bureau of Labor Statistics, 2014a). Although Hispanics make up 16 percent of the total CLF, they make up 20 percent of the unemployed CLF (U.S. Congress Joint Economic Committee, 2013).

Many agencies, including DoD, prefer to hire people who have a minimum of a high school education. Among Hispanics 25 years of age and older in the CLF, 71 percent had completed high school, while 90 percent or more of whites, blacks, and Asians had done so (U.S. Bureau of Labor Statistics, 2014a). Across most education levels, Hispanics have higher unemployment rates than the total CLF (see Figure 2.2) (U.S. Bureau of Labor Statistics, 2014a). The one exception is among those with less than a high school education, such that Hispanics in that group are less likely to be unemployed than the total CLF.

Hispanics in 2013 were most concentrated in service occupations, with 27 percent working in such fields as health care support, protective service, food preparation, building and grounds cleaning, and personal care and service (Figure 2.3) (U.S. Bureau of Labor Statistics, 2014a). Hispanics were less represented than others in managerial positions and more represented in production and transportation and construction and maintenance professions. Hispanic men were most likely to work in construction and maintenance occupations, while Hispanic women were most likely to work in ser-

Figure 2.2
Hispanic Civilian Labor Force and Total Civilian Labor Force Unemployment Rates, by Education Level

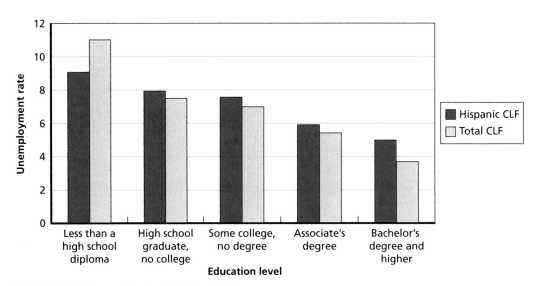

SOURCE: U.S. Bureau of Labor Statistics, 2014a.
RAND *RR1699-2.2*

Figure 2.3
Occupation Distribution for the Total Labor Force and the Hispanic Labor Force

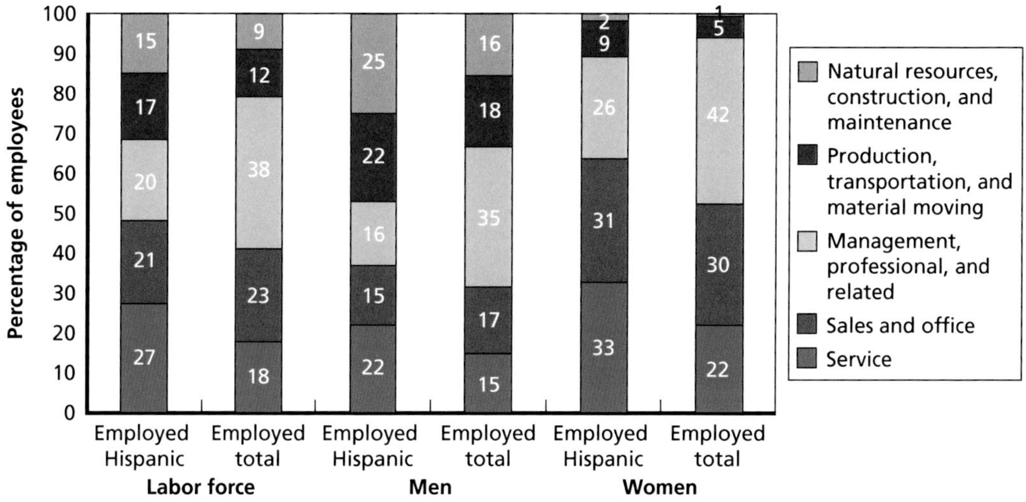

SOURCE: U.S. Bureau of Labor Statistics, 2014a.
NOTE: Numbers might not add to 100 because of rounding.
RAND RR1699-2.3

vice occupations. Foreign-born Hispanics in 2012 were more likely than native-born Hispanics to work in service occupations but less likely to work in management and professional occupations (Mosisa, 2013).

Summary

In many reports, including those that EEOC requires, people who identify as Hispanic are counted as Hispanic, regardless of racial-group identification. All those who are not Hispanic are classified based on their racial-group identification. Confusion regarding race, ethnicity, and Hispanic origin might contribute to variation in reporting of race and ethnicity over time.

Determining overall characteristics of the Hispanic workforce is important for comparisons addressing how federal-agency workforces fare in employing Hispanic workers. For example, if a workforce does not operate in certain locations or has a limited diversity of occupations, those limitations might influence the extent to which that workforce is of interest to Hispanics in the CLF. The Hispanic population in the United States is increasing and is expected to continue doing so for the next several decades. In the CLF, Hispanics have higher unemployment rates than other groups, differences that persist across most levels of education. In addition, Hispanics in the CLF are most likely to work in service occupations.

CHAPTER THREE

Application of Prior Guidance and Analytic Efforts to Hispanic Employment in the Department of Defense

Title VII, Section 717 of the Civil Rights Act of 1964 establishes that U.S. executive agencies and military departments (excluding uniformed members) must annually review their affirmative action programs for EEO on the basis of race, color, religion, sex, and national origin. Section 717 also establishes that EEOC is responsible for reviewing and approving the affirmative action programs and operations of each federal executive agency and military department. EEOC has provided subsequent guidance to federal entities to help develop and evaluate these programs. In this chapter, we review prior guidance and then conduct corresponding analyses addressing Hispanic representation in DoD.

Prior Guidance and Analytic Efforts Addressing Barrier Analyses

EEOC uses EEO MD-715 to communicate affirmative action program standards to federal agencies and establish reporting requirements for these entities. EEO MD-715 outlines six core elements for a model Title VII program and provides several attributes and actions that these programs should incorporate. The core elements are as follows (EEO MD-715):

1. *demonstrated commitment* by agency leaders to EEO for Hispanics
2. *EEO integration* into agency structure, mission, and operations
3. *management and accountability*, including policies and procedures that hold managers, supervisors, and EEO officials accountable for the agency's Title VII program
4. *proactive prevention* of discrimination and elimination of barriers to employment
5. *efficiency and fairness* in processes for tracking and resolving EEO disputes and complaints
6. *legal compliance* with EEOC regulations, orders, and instructions.

Element 4, proactive prevention, addresses the identification and subsequent elimination of employment barriers for different demographic groups, including Hispanics.

EEOC provides detailed information on the self-assessments that agencies should conduct to address these core elements and identify potential employment barriers. Specifically, Part A of EEO MD-715 instructs federal executive agencies and military departments (excluding uniformed personnel) to review their workforce characteristics annually to identify possible barriers to the employment of certain groups, including Hispanics, in the agencies' workforces. To determine whether barriers might be present, EEOC requires that agencies perform a workforce data analysis involving numerical data on employee characteristics (EEOC, 2004). EEOC notes that this analysis should use a series of workforce "snapshots," which should include data that are divided by race, national origin, and sex (see online Appendix B). The snapshots can guide evaluations of group representation.

Evaluation of Workforce Data

Evaluation of whether an agency has adequate participation and representation rates of Hispanics necessitates comparison with standard rates. EEOC requires that federal agencies compare their rates with rates from a benchmark population. Underrepresentation, as defined in 5 CFR § 720.202, exists when the number of women or members of a minority group within a category of civil service employment constitutes a lower percentage of the total number of employees within the employment category than the percentage of women or the minority group constitutes within the CLF of the United States. Thus, the rates for the benchmark population come from the relevant CLF. For federal agencies, EEOC's EEO MD-715 tables use only those who are U.S. citizens. For private entities, the tables include both those who are and those who are not U.S. citizens. To further address the issue of conducting comparisons with only the relevant CLF, an agency might compare Hispanic representation within a particular occupation in that agency with Hispanic representation seen in that occupation in the CLF, rather than considering only total agency representation and total CLF representation of Hispanics. Agencies can also consider geographic location in their analyses, such that they might compare the agency's Hispanic representation with Hispanic representation in the metropolitan area in which the agency is located. However, if an agency's workforce is not centralized, it might be more appropriate to use nationwide data.

If agencies find lower rates of representation and participation for Hispanics than are evident in the relevant CLF (EEOC, 2004), barriers to Hispanic employment might exist. If agencies find discrepancies indicating possible workforce barriers, EEOC requires them to conduct more in-depth assessments into the potential causes for these discrepancies (EEOC, 2014). The in-depth assessments might include review of information pertinent to the triggers, review of agency reports and documents, and consultation with people who might have knowledge about the sources of the triggers. Following these additional assessments into the root causes for triggers, agencies should devise targeted action plans to address employment barriers. EEOC requires each agency to provide a report of its plans and progress each year.

Determination of whether a discrepancy is sufficiently large to trigger further analyses depends, in part, on an EEOC reviewer's discretion (EEOC, 2014). Different federal agencies have different workforce structures, sizes, locations, occupations, and other characteristics. It can be challenging to standardize an approach or set of approaches appropriate to use in assessing the magnitude of representation discrepancies between, for example, representation of all groups across all agencies and that seen in the relevant CLF. Therefore, EEOC does not provide a standard rule of thumb for agencies to use when comparing representation within their workforces with representation seen in the CLF. As discussed below, the lack of a standard rule of thumb or complementary set of rules of thumb can contribute to confusion among agencies when they are evaluating the magnitude of their own discrepancies. In addition, the absence of a standard rule of thumb or set of rules of thumb might lead different reviewers to come to different conclusions regarding the presence of employment barriers when evaluating the same workforce data.

Assessment of Discrepancies

Below, we describe possible rules of thumb to determine the presence of discrepancies, or representation triggers. It was outside the scope of the current project to collect and evaluate all potential rules of thumb that could be used for evaluating the magnitude of a representation discrepancy. A working group of practitioners, social and behavioral scientists, and representatives from federal agencies might be able to establish more-definitive rules of thumb for federal agencies to use when evaluating representation discrepancies, which could provide agencies with much-needed guidance in this area.

None of the rules of thumb we describe is without fault, and there is no universally accepted assessment or combination of assessments for identifying the presence of large discrepancies in employment rates (Greenberg, 1979; Peresie, 2009; Roth, Bobko, and Switzer, 2006). Some might consider the following rules of thumb arbitrary (Gold, 1985). For example, when using rules of thumb for determining employment discrepancies, a value that falls below a cutoff might be considered to show a substantial disparity, regardless of whether that value is only slightly below the cutoff or far below the cutoff (Mead and Morris, 2011). Further, tests of statistical significance are sensitive to sample size (Peresie, 2009). Although we review and consider these rules, we do not endorse them as stand-alone evidence of the presence of employment barriers. Rather, readers and practitioners should interpret these rules of thumb as data points in an analysis, not as final determinations of the presence or absence of employment barriers.

Certain rules of thumb—namely, the 80-percent rule of thumb and two–standard deviation rule of thumb—are frequently used in the context of establishing the presence of adverse or disparate impact within an agency (Kaye, 1983; Morris and Lobsenz, 2000). Adverse or disparate impact occurs when employment practices, such as hiring and promotion, have a disadvantageous effect on members of protected groups, regardless of whether this effect was intended (EEOC, 1979).[1] These rules of thumb are used less frequently to compare the representation of a group within an agency (e.g., DoD) with the representation of that group in a larger labor force (e.g., CLF; but see R. Biddle, 1995, for example legal cases and Sobol and Ellard, 1988, for a population-to-workforce ratio discussion). These rules are thus more often used for comparing demographic differences in selection rates than for assessing representation rates. In the absence of legislated or widely used rules of thumb for comparisons between an agency's group representation and that group's representation in a larger labor force, we draw from these available rules of thumb to illustrate how rules of thumb could be used for such comparisons. However, we acknowledge that application of these rules of thumb to this particular context is not ideal. EEOC-supported rules of thumb for use by federal agencies to evaluate the magnitude of agency representation discrepancies with the relevant CLF would be most helpful for use in this context, but, given that these do not exist, we consider rules of thumb frequently used in other contexts. We also acknowledge that various other rules from the adverse-impact analysis literature could be considered for extension to this context or that new rules could be developed for use in this context (e.g., D. Biddle and Morris, 2011; Kadane, 1990).

Any-Discrepancy Rule of Thumb

The any-discrepancy rule of thumb highlights and responds to any observed discrepancy in employment rates between one group and others. As noted previously, EEOC utilizes this rule when evaluating discrepancies between a group's representation in an agency and that group's representation in the CLF, allowing for some slight discrepancies. The any-discrepancy rule does not explicitly consider the size of representation discrepancies. By chance, one would expect some variation in employment rates among groups, such as slight discrepancies between an agency's group representation and that group's representation in the CLF, and one might also expect variation in group representation during different time periods or seasons. The any-discrepancy rule would flag a discrepancy if, for example, Hispanic citizens were to make up 10 percent of the CLF but only 9.5 percent of an agency's workforce. Yet, the extent to which such a discrepancy is larger than would be expected by chance is unclear. That is, it is not clear that this 0.5-percent discrepancy indicates meaningful differences between groups in representation. If agencies utilize this any-discrepancy rule of thumb, they might devote multiple resources to address a representation discrepancy that might not be practically or statistically meaningful.

---

[1] If adverse impact appears to be present, employers generally must conduct validity studies to address whether policies or practices are job-related or business necessities. If a policy or practice is not valid, the employer must change the procedures and practices in place. Overall, employers must make reasonable efforts to find and use procedures and practices that minimize adverse impact.

The 80-Percent Rule of Thumb

Within the federal guidelines addressing employment discrimination is 29 CFR § 1607.4(D), which describes a general 80-percent, or four-fifths, rule of thumb to use when evaluating agency selection rates for different demographic groups, including racial and ethnic groups. Using this rule of thumb, a selection rate for one racial or ethnic group that is less than 80 percent of that for another group (i.e., the group with the highest selection ratio) would indicate a barrier.

This rule of thumb is frequently used to establish the presence of disparate, or adverse, impact within a workforce, and U.S. General Accounting Office, 2003, and U.S. Government Accountability Office, 2005, use this rule to evaluate adverse impact within workforce data from federal agencies. EEOC, 1979, however, cautions,

> This "4/5ths" or "80%" rule of thumb is not intended as a legal definition, but is a practical means of keeping the attention of the enforcement agencies on serious discrepancies in rates of hiring, promotion and other selection decisions. (Question 11, Section II, Adverse Impact, the Bottom Line and Affirmative Action)

Although it might provide some guidance to agencies when evaluating their workforce snapshots, this rule has been criticized for being ambiguous, having low reliability, and placing greater demand on smaller employers (McKinley, 2008; Sobol and Ellard, 1988). Many courts have disregarded this rule when assessing whether an agency has an unlawful employment barrier in place (e.g., McKinley, 2008; Mitchell, 2013). However, agencies might consider this rule of thumb as one data point, or one example, in a larger analysis.

Two–Standard Deviation Rule of Thumb

Individuals, agencies, and courts have also used a two–standard deviation rule of thumb to identify possible adverse or disparate impact (e.g., Kaye, 1983). The standard deviation is a statistical value that measures the dispersion of a variable, so this rule seeks to use statistical information about a selection rate to evaluate the size of a discrepancy. Using this rule of thumb, a selection rate for one racial or ethnic group that is two standard deviations from that of a reference group would indicate a possible barrier.[2]

Although seemingly simple, this rule can be very difficult to apply. Some entities have substituted standard errors, which measure variability of an estimated rate and depend on the sample size, for standard deviations in their analysis. However, these analyses give large organizations a narrower window for compliance because they have more data on which to draw. Jacobs, Deckert, and Silva, 2011, therefore recommend the use of procedures that are truly dependent on standard deviations. Although such

---

[2]   As mentioned previously, this rule is less frequently used in comparisons between a workforce (e.g., DoD) and a larger labor market (e.g., CLF) than for comparisons within a workforce.

methods are available (and Jacobs, Deckert, and Silva, 2011, recommend two), applying these methods to test for barriers in the federal employment process still requires specification of how large of a standardized discrepancy constitutes a barrier. These application difficulties can multiply in arenas (such as courts) in which there might be limited familiarity or knowledge of statistics. Lack of familiarity with and understanding of statistical concepts, including the influence of sample sizes, creates confusion and hinders decisionmakers' ability to assess whether large discrepancies are present. There have been instances within the adverse-impact context in which use of the 80-percent and the two–standard deviation rule on the same data yield different conclusions on whether meaningful discrepancies are present (Jacobs, Deckert, and Silva, 2011; Peresie, 2009).

Statistical Significance Versus Practical Significance

In assessing discrepancies in data, social scientists distinguish between *statistical significance* and *practical significance*. A difference in selection rates or representation rates is statistically significant when the difference can be confidently distinguished from statistical noise. This depends on the size of both the difference and the sample (because larger samples produce more-precise estimates with less noise). The two–standard deviation rule of thumb is essentially a test of statistical significance.

In comparing large groups (such as DoD civilian workers and the CLF), tiny differences in rates can be estimated precisely enough to meet the criteria for statistical significance without being meaningful enough to warrant an investigation of potential barriers. In other words, statistically significant differences might not be practically significant.

In comparisons between small groups, large and meaningful differences in rates might not be statistically significant (i.e., they might pass the two–standard deviation rule), but they might still merit further investigation. That is, practically significant differences might not be statistically significant. The 80-percent rule of thumb might be considered a test of practical significance. The two–standard deviation rule and the 80-percent rule can be complementary. For this reason, others have recommended using both practical and statistical significance tests in adverse-impact analyses (Dunleavy, 2010).

Other Common Triggers

Other common triggers, suggesting the presence of barriers, include the following (EEOC, 2014):[3]

- In *low entry–high exit*, a group with a low rate of participation in the total workforce enters the workforce at a low rate but exits it at a high rate. This might occur if Hispanics are hired at low rates but separate at high rates.
- In *glass wall*, a group has relatively low representation in occupations that are tracked for upward mobility. This might occur if Hispanics have low rates of participation in and hiring into certain upwardly mobile occupations.
- In *blocked pipeline*, a group has a low rate of promotion within certain occupations. This might occur if Hispanics have lower promotion rates than others in occupations that are upwardly mobile.
- In *glass ceiling*, a group has a low rate of participation in and promotion into leadership positions. This might occur if Hispanics have low representation within senior grades and a low rate of promotion into these grades.

Limitations in Applicant Information

In addition to the CLF data previously reviewed, DoD has a source of applicant data it can analyze to determine whether Hispanics are hired at lower rates than others. This is OPM's online job board, USAJOBS.gov, the federal government's official site for job postings (USAJOBS, undated). This site permits agencies to advertise jobs to interested people across the nation. When applying for positions, an applicant can, but is not required to, provide information regarding demographic characteristics, including race and ethnicity. USAJOBS is the primary source of applicant information for federal agencies, but, as we later discuss, its information is limited. We utilize applicant and application data later in this report, but, as discussed in Chapter Five, limitations with these data can make it difficult for agencies to complete EEOC workforce data tables that involve applicant flow.

---

[3] EEOC, 2014, recommends assessment of these triggers within federal workforces. Given that they include assessments of differences in selection rates, several of these analyses align with more-typical adverse-impact analyses. For example, to determine adverse impact in promotion, an analyst might compare the promotion rate of the group of interest (e.g., Hispanics) with the promotion rate of the group with the highest selection rate (e.g., non-Hispanic whites).

Application to Department of Defense Hispanic Employment Barrier Analyses

We now apply analyses to DoD and its components (Air Force, Army, Navy, and Fourth Estate).[4] In doing so, we exclude noncitizens from analyses, given that U.S. citizenship is a requirement for federal employment. Our analyses use data from several sources, including OPM data on all federal employees and detailed characteristics of their employment from 2008 to 2013, as well as statistics on the CLF from the ACS. We provide additional analyses in online Appendixes C and D that further compare Hispanic employees and non-Hispanic employees in DoD and examine Hispanic representation in several occupations.

Overall Hispanic Representation in the Federal Workforce, Department of Defense Civilian Workforce, and Civilian Labor Force

Hispanic representation in the DoD civilian workforce has been lower than in both the non-DoD federal civilian workforce and the total CLF in recent years (see Figure 3.1). In 2013, the most recent year for which data are available, 6.5 percent of DoD employees were Hispanic, as were 9.3 percent of the federal civilian workforce and 11.4 percent of the relevant CLF (i.e., excluding noncitizens). Hispanic representation in the CLF has grown more rapidly in recent years than it has in the federal workforces.

Hispanic representation differs across the individual DoD services, as shown in Figure 3.2. In 2013, the Department of the Army had the highest level of Hispanic representation within DoD, at 7.4 percent, but still lagged behind the levels of representation in the non-DoD federal workforce and in the CLF.[5] Other services had levels of representation that were below average for DoD, with the Fourth Estate—which, for our purposes, consists of DoD entities not in the military departments or combatant commands—having the lowest level, at 5.2 percent.

DoD Fourth Estate agencies vary in their levels of Hispanic representation. Figure 3.3 shows Hispanic representation from 2008 to 2013 in the three largest Fourth Estate agencies, which are DCMA, DLA, and DFAS. DLA and DCMA had

---

[4] The Fourth Estate in this context includes the following agencies: Defense Acquisition University, Defense Advanced Research Projects Agency, Defense Commissary Agency, Defense Contract Audit Agency, Defense Contract Management Agency (DCMA), Defense Finance and Accounting Service (DFAS), Defense Health Agency, Defense Human Resource Activity, Defense Information Systems Agency, Defense Legal Services Agency, Defense Logistics Agency (DLA), Defense Media Activity, Defense Microelectronics Activity, Defense POW/MIA Accounting Agency, Defense Security Cooperation Agency, Defense Security Service, Defense Technical Information Center, Defense Technology Security Administration, Defense Threat Reduction Agency, DoD Education Activity, DoD Office of Inspector General, Joint Staff, Missile Defense Agency, National Defense University, Office of Economic Adjustment, OSD, Pentagon Force Protection Agency, U.S. Court of Appeals for the Armed Forces, and Washington Headquarters Services. We follow EEOC procedure for calculations involving the CLF. Because of this, we exclude noncitizens.

[5] We also considered the influence of veteran status and found that Hispanics make up about 6 percent of veterans in the CLF and about 7 percent of veterans working for DoD.

Figure 3.1
Hispanic Representation in the Civilian Labor Force, Non–Department of Defense Federal Civilian Workforce, and Department of Defense Civilian Workforce

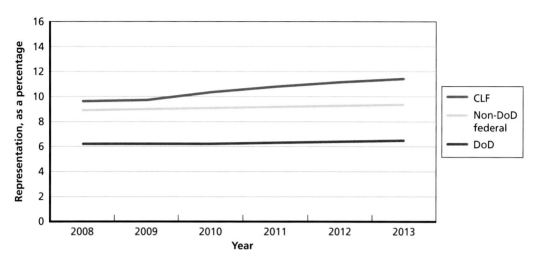

SOURCES: ACS and OPM data.
NOTE: The 2013 levels of representation, as well as the increases between 2008 and 2013, are all statistically distinguishable from one another at the 0.05 level.
RAND RR1699-3.1

Figure 3.2
Hispanic Representation in the Civilian Labor Force Versus Department of Defense Components

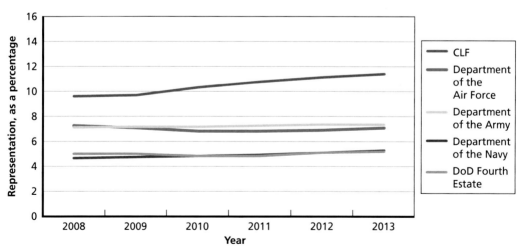

SOURCES: ACS and OPM data.
NOTE: All component differences are statistically significant at the 0.05 level, except for the differences between the Navy and the Fourth Estate.
RAND RR1699-3.2

Figure 3.3
Hispanic Representation in the Three Largest Fourth Estate Agencies

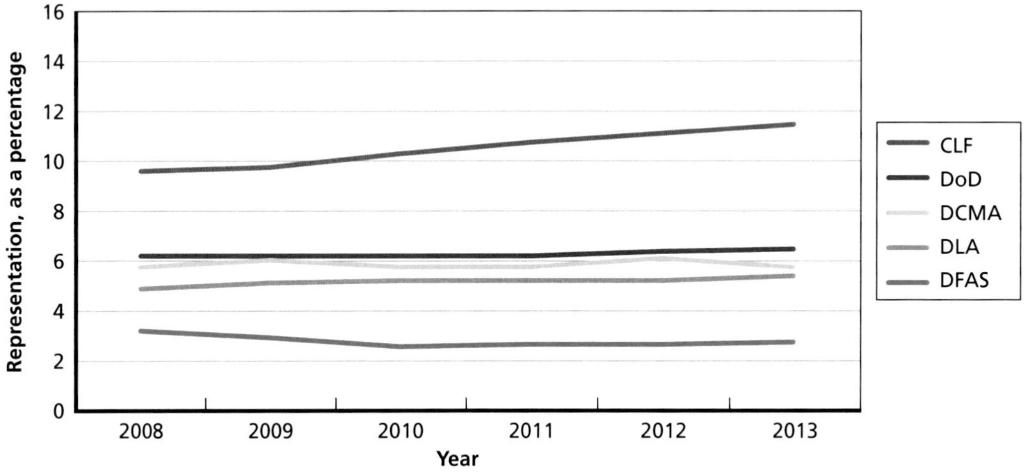

SOURCES: ACS and OPM data.
NOTE: The three largest Fourth Estate agencies are DLA, DFAS, and DCMA. Differences between the overall DoD level of representation and the level in each Fourth Estate agency are statistically significant.
RAND *RR1699-3.3*

levels of Hispanic representation close to (though still below) the overall level in DoD, but representation in DFAS was significantly lower (less than 3 percent).

Assessing the Significance of Discrepancies in Representation

The discrepancies between Hispanic representation in federal and other workforces are significant according to different rules of thumb.[6]

Any-Discrepancy Rule of Thumb

The strictest standard for evaluating discrepancies is the any-discrepancy rule of thumb, which considers all discrepancies noteworthy, regardless of their magnitude. As is evident in Figures 3.1 and 3.2, DoD and the non-DoD federal workforces do not meet this standard: Each has lower representation of Hispanic workers than is evident in the CLF. Further, each DoD component also has lower representation of Hispanic workers than is evident in the CLF.

The 80-Percent Rule of Thumb

Applying the 80-percent (or four-fifths) rule of thumb to this context, we find a difference between Hispanic representation in the DoD civilian workforce and that in the CLF. Hispanics make up 11.4 percent of the CLF (excluding noncitizens), as indicated by the red line in Figure 3.4. Four-fifths of this level is 9.1 percent, indicated by the

---

[6]   As noted previously, the 80-percent rule of thumb and two–standard deviation rule of thumb are typically used in the context of adverse-impact analyses.

Figure 3.4
2013 Hispanic Representation Versus the Civilian Labor Force and 80-Percent Rule of Thumb

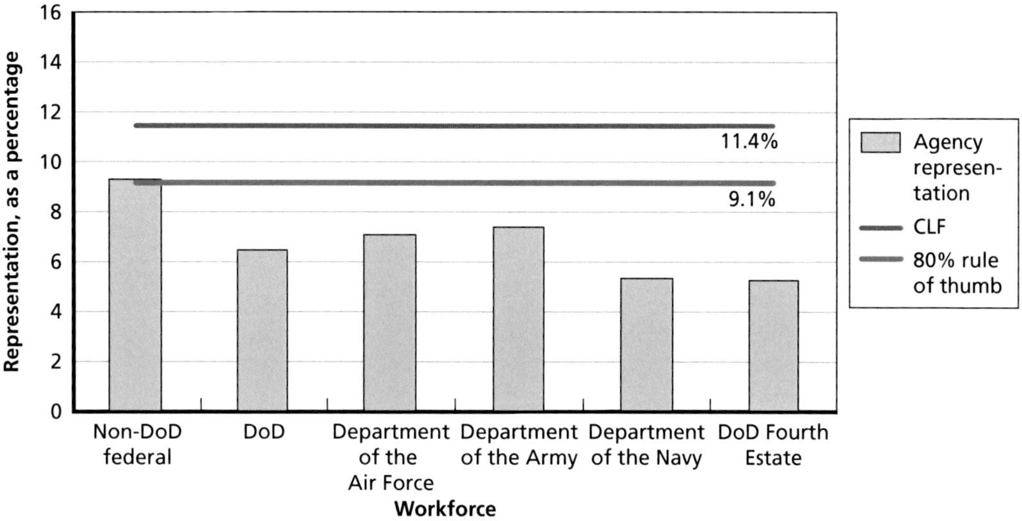

SOURCES: ACS and OPM data.
RAND RR1699-3.4

blue line in Figure 3.4. Both DoD overall and each of its components fall below the four-fifths threshold, although the non-DoD federal workforce meets it.

Two–Standard Deviation Rule of Thumb

Applying the two–standard deviation rule to this context, the sheer sizes of the CLF and DoD workforces mean that this standard will indicate virtually any shortfall in Hispanic representation of the DoD workforce as a discrepancy. This is because variability in an estimated rate, as mentioned earlier in this chapter, is much smaller in large samples. In populations the size of DoD and the CLF, a two–standard deviation difference amounts to less than 0.1 percent in the employment rate of Hispanics. The differences shown in Figure 3.2 are many standard deviations from the representation of Hispanic citizens in the CLF, which indicates that the differences are measured with enough precision to distinguish them from random noise—that is, they are statistically significant.

Other Common Triggers

Additional common triggers also indicate potential barriers to Hispanic employment in DoD. In this section, we review results of analyses using low entry–high exit, glass-wall, blocked-pipeline, and glass-ceiling triggers. There are several additional ways beyond those described in this chapter to operationalize these triggers. Rather than provide multiple, overlapping analyses in this chapter, we instead present a core set of analyses and refer the reader to online Appendix C for additional analyses.

Low Entry–High Exit

A low entry–high exit pattern is present when representation is higher among person-nel separating from the organization than among new hires. This is true of Hispanics in the DoD civilian workforce: They made up 5.2 percent of new hires but 6.0 percent of separations from 2008 to 2013.[7] The overall pattern of low entry–high exit stems from the Air Force and DoD Fourth Estate agencies, in which Hispanic employees made up 5.0 percent and 3.9 percent of new hires, while representation among separa-tions was 6.8 percent and 5.0 percent, respectively, suggesting that retention factors are particularly important for these agencies to consider. Hispanic representation among new hires was approximately equal to representation among separations for the Army and Navy. All else equal, the aggregate pattern means that the overall level of Hispanic representation in DoD will decrease over time.

Glass Wall

A glass wall is present when a group is underrepresented in occupations that are tracked for upward mobility—thereby limiting group members' upward mobility over time. To assess this trigger, we examine ethnic differences in rates of participation in high-promoting occupations.

To determine which occupations are high promoting, we consider two metrics: high rates of promotion to subsequent grade levels and high rates of mobility into supervisory positions from nonsupervisory positions. We chose cutoff rates for each metric that ensured that approximately 5 to 10 percent of DoD employees would be classified as being in high-promoting areas. For an occupation to be high promoting according to the grade-level standard, more than 25 percent of workers in it must move to a higher grade each year. For an occupation to be high promoting under the super-visory standard, more than 5 percent of workers in it must move from nonsupervisory to supervisory positions each year. In both cases, we include all DoD employees, not just those who remained within the same agency. For example, employees who are promoted and change agencies count toward the promotion rate for their occupations. Online Appendix D provides additional information regarding high-promoting occu-pations by agency.

Figure 3.5 shows the results of the glass-wall analysis under each metric for DoD as a whole (though similar patterns exist in each individual component). By both metrics—high rates of mobility into higher grades and high rates of movement from nonsupervisory to supervisory positions—Hispanics have lower rates of participation in high-promoting occupations. Both differences shown in the figure are statistically significant and, when we apply the 80-percent rule of thumb to this context, suggest

---

[7]   To further explore the exit rates of Hispanics, we compared their exit rates with those of non-Hispanics, rather than their proportion among exiting employees. From 2008 to 2013, 6.5 percent of Hispanics left each year, whereas 6.7 percent of non-Hispanics left each year.

Figure 3.5
Percentage of Hispanic and Non-Hispanic Employees in High-Promoting Occupations, 2009–2013

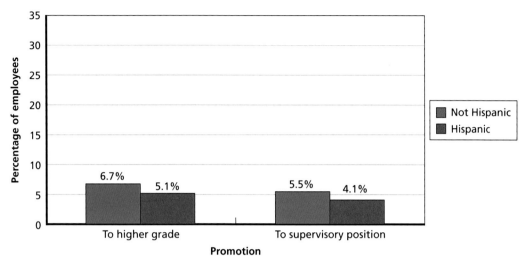

SOURCE: OPM data.
NOTE: Both differences between Hispanic and non-Hispanic employees are statistically significant.
RAND RR1699-3.5

practical significance as well. In short, Hispanic employees in DoD are less likely than others to work in high-promoting occupations.

Blocked Pipeline

Not only are Hispanics less likely to work in high-promoting occupations; those who do work in such occupations are less likely to be promoted than others. That is, they face what EEOC calls a blocked pipeline. Figure 3.6 shows promotion rates in the high-promoting occupations (as defined earlier) for Hispanic and non-Hispanic employees. In both occupations with high levels of advancement to subsequent pay grades and those with high levels of advancement to supervisory roles, Hispanics are less likely to be promoted than non-Hispanics. Although these differences are statistically significant, they fall short of the 80-percent rule of thumb. Similar patterns, in which Hispanic employees in high-promoting occupations are slightly less likely to be promoted, exist in the individual DoD components. Further analyses in online Appendix C show little overall difference in promotion rates by either metric outside high-promoting occupations.

Glass Ceiling

The final trigger that could indicate a barrier to Hispanic employment in DoD is known as a glass ceiling. This exists when a group has a low rate of participation in leadership positions relative to their overall participation in the organization.

Figure 3.6
Average Promotion Rates, by Ethnicity, in High-Promoting Occupations, 2009–2013

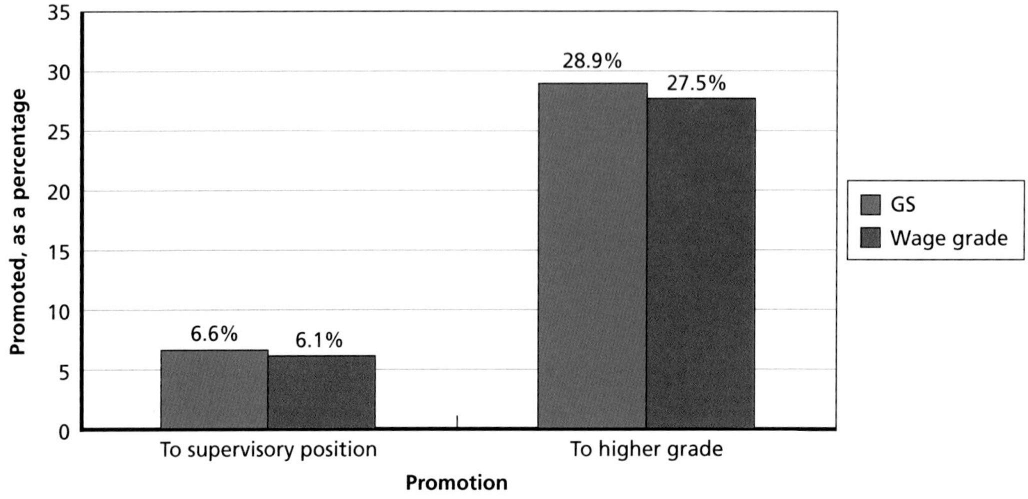

SOURCE: OPM data.
NOTE: Both differences between Hispanic and non-Hispanic employees are statistically significant.
RAND RR1699-3.6

Capturing the glass-ceiling effect first requires a way to partition the organization into different levels of leadership. We begin by comparing overall Hispanic representation in General Schedule (GS) grades (which consist primarily of white-collar occupations) with Hispanic representation in wage grades (which consist of blue-collar occupations).[8] Figure 3.7 shows this comparison for DoD as a whole and separately by component. It shows that Hispanics are more represented in wage grades than in GS grades in DoD, as well as three of its components, but that they are more represented in GS grades in non-DoD federal agencies and the Department of the Navy. Put another way, this figure shows that there might be a glass ceiling for Hispanics in DoD but not in other federal agencies.

A second way to test for a glass ceiling is to examine representation at different pay grades within GS positions. Figure 3.8 shows how Hispanic representation in each grade compares with overall representation in the GS echelon. The bars illustrate the grade-specific representation levels, while the dashed line represents the overall level of representation in the grades depicted in the figure. For example, the first bar on the left depicts a value of 9.3 percent, which is above the level of 6.5 percent for all GS grades, indicating that Hispanic employees are disproportionately represented in the GS-4 grade relative to the overall level. Finally, although Figure 3.8 shows an aggregate view

---

[8]   Senior Executive Service (SES) positions utilize a unique hiring structure and make up only 0.2 percent of positions in the DoD civilian workforce. Therefore, we do not provide analyses addressing these positions.

Figure 3.7
Hispanic Representation in General Schedule and Wage-Grade Positions, 2013

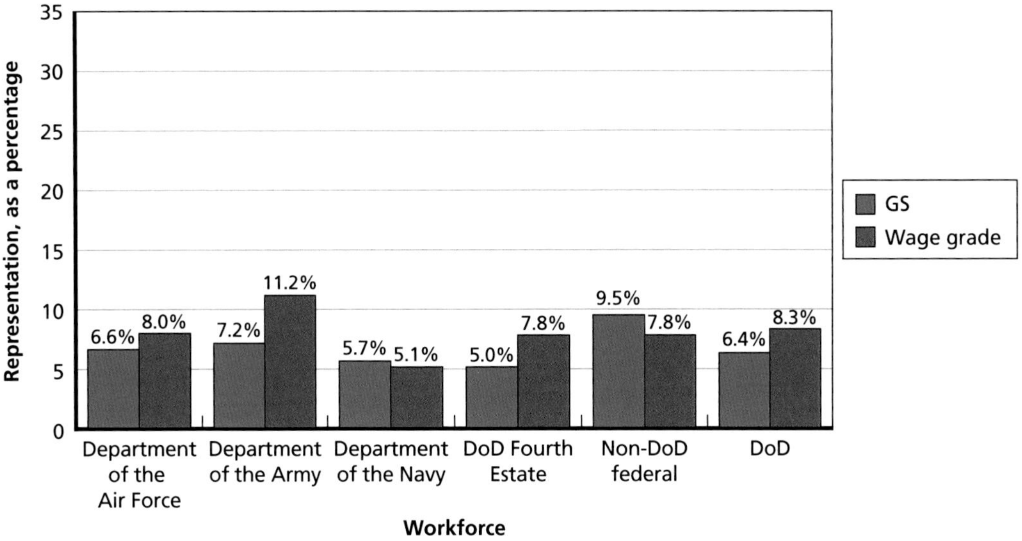

SOURCE: OPM data.
NOTE: Differences between the proportion of Hispanics in non-DoD GS grades and that in GS grades in DoD and each of its components are statistically significant. Differences between proportion of Hispanics in non-DoD wage grades and those in Army, Navy, and overall DoD wage grades are also statistically significant.
RAND *RR1699-3.7*

of all DoD GS employees, the patterns are generally similar to those that exist in the individual components.

The patterns in Figure 3.8 indicate that DoD's Hispanic employees are not evenly distributed across GS pay grades; rather, representation declines as GS pay grade increases. The representation levels behind the numbers in Figure 3.8 show that this pattern is particularly pronounced among the highest levels of GS employees—grades 12 through 15. In the lowest tier, grades 4 through 10, Hispanic representation is 8.0 percent. In the middle tier, grades 11 and 12, it is 6.0 percent. In the top tier, grades 13 through 15, it is 4.5 percent. To the degree that the upper tier of GS grades feeds the highest levels of leadership, this glass-ceiling effect could limit Hispanic representation among senior DoD civilian leaders.

Glass Ceiling in Hiring

A related glass ceiling might operate through outside hiring because Hispanic employees are underrepresented among new hires to top positions. Figure 3.9, similar to Figure 3.8 but limited to newly hired employees, indicates that Hispanic representation also tends to decline as GS grade increases among new hires, with grades 12 through 15 deviating most from the overall level of representation. As before, Figure 3.9 presents the overall view of DoD, but patterns in the individual components are similar.

Figure 3.8
Hispanic Representation in Each General Schedule Grade Versus Overall Representation, 2009–2013

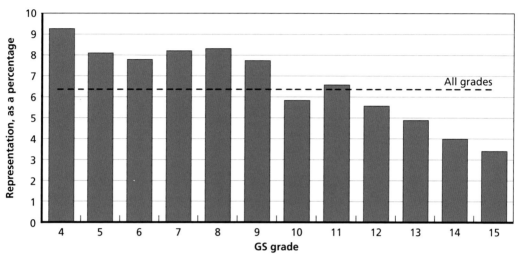

SOURCE: OPM data.
NOTE: The differences in representation across grade levels are statistically significant. This figure shows grade-specific representation levels, but the reader should also bear in mind that the grades differ in size. Thus, the underrepresentation in grades 12–13 amounts to more people in numerical terms than the underrepresentation in grades 14–15, which is considerably smaller.
RAND RR1699-3.8

In summary, for the data behind Figure 3.9 using the same categories as before, Hispanic employees make up 6.1 percent of new hires in the lower grades (GS-4 to GS-10), 4.1 percent of new hires in the middle grades (GS-11 and GS-12), and 2.8 percent of new hires in upper grades (GS-13 to GS-15). All else being equal, this pattern of hiring will create a workforce in which Hispanic employees are concentrated in lower-grade positions.

Summary

Hispanic representation in DoD lags behind that of the CLF and the rest of the federal government. We applied different rules of thumb to evaluate the data. These rules of thumb each served as one piece of information addressing whether there might be employment barriers for Hispanics in DoD. Using these rules of thumb, our analyses indicate that the DoD representation gap is both statistically and practically significant. When evaluating their own workforce data, agency analysts might also consider several rules of thumb to determine whether barriers to employment are present within their agencies. Our analyses also indicate that this representation gap is unlikely to improve: Hispanic representation is higher among separating employees than among

Figure 3.9
Hispanic Representation in Each General Schedule Grade Versus Overall Representation Among New Hires, 2009–2013

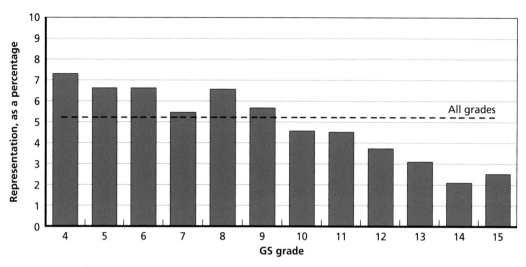

SOURCE: OPM data.
NOTE: The differences in representation across grade levels are statistically significant.
RAND RR1699-3.9

new hires, Hispanics are less likely to work in high-promoting areas and are concentrated in lower-grade positions. Later in this report, we describe interviews we conducted to address potential perceptions that might contribute to discrepancies. In addition, survey data, such as those available through the Federal Employee Viewpoint Survey, might also provide helpful information regarding employee perceptions. We turn next to possible workforce characteristics that might cause these differences.

CHAPTER FOUR

Analyzing Differences in Hispanic Representation Across Labor Forces

Identifying and eliminating barriers to Hispanic employment in DoD requires understanding the root causes of representation gaps. In this chapter, we explore the extent to which observable differences, such as those regarding the types of jobs available, education requirements, and job locations, can explain why Hispanic employees are underrepresented in DoD. These analyses build from those shown in Chapter Three by further exploring what factors account for the difference in overall Hispanic representation in the DoD workforce and that seen in the CLF and non-DoD federal workforce.

We find that observable differences in workforce characteristics can account for most of the Hispanic representation gap in DoD relative to the CLF, as well as most of that between the DoD and the non-DoD federal workforce. Differences in education levels, citizenship, veteran status, age, occupation types, and location each contribute roughly 1 to 2 percentage points to the gap in Hispanic representation seen between DoD and the CLF. Comparisons between DoD and the non-DoD federal workforce indicate that differences in locations and occupation types can account for the representation gap, but these effects are partly offset by differences in education levels and federal job categories, which favor DoD Hispanic representation.

We begin by summarizing the differences among DoD, non-DoD federal, and all civilian workers, using OPM and ACS data to do so. We briefly describe how to interpret the results from these analyses, known as Blinder–Oaxaca decomposition analyses, and then present the results of these analyses comparing DoD with the CLF and with the non-DoD federal workforce. We conclude with a discussion of the policy implications of our results. In online Appendix E, we provide a detailed discussion of the Blinder–Oaxaca decomposition methodology.

Data and Descriptive Statistics

As in Chapter Three, we use OPM data on all full-time nonseasonal federal civilian workers and ACS data on all civilian workers in 2013. We include noncitizens in our CLF sample, which differs from the analysis done in Chapter Three. Notably, the analysis in Chapter Three was intended to mirror the analysis that EEOC recommends, which excludes noncitizens. We chose to keep noncitizens in the analyses presented in this chapter because that allows us to examine the impact that the government policy of employing only citizens has on Hispanic representation in DoD.

Characteristics of Each Workforce

Table 4.1 delineates the key individual and job characteristics we observe for each worker in our data.[1] Column 1 provides the summary statistics for workers in the DoD workforce, column 2 provides such statistics for the CLF, and column 3 provides them for the non-DoD federal workforce. Hispanics are the only racial/ethnic group that is less represented among DoD civilian employees than in the CLF.[2]

Several other differences are also evident between DoD workers and all CLF individuals. DoD workers are more likely to be citizens or veterans.[3] These differences are to be expected because DoD employs only citizens and gives various hiring preferences to veterans. The average DoD worker is also more likely to be male, older, and more educated than all CLF workers. DoD jobs are also more likely to be professional, administrative, or technical and less likely to be clerical and blue collar than those in the CLF. DoD workers are slightly more likely to be located in metropolitan areas.[4]

DoD workers also differ from non-DoD federal workers. DoD employees are more likely to be male, older, and veterans than their non-DoD counterparts, but they also tend to be less educated. In addition, compared with the non-DoD federal workforce, DoD has a greater proportion of blue-collar jobs and a greater proportion belonging to the competitive service.

---

[1]   In addition to the variables described in Table 4.1, we observe a few others that we did not include in the table for brevity reasons but that we did use in the analysis. For both the OPM and ACS data, we observe the state in which the person resides. Additional variables that are available for OPM data include a two-digit occupation code that classifies workers into 59 categories according to their areas of specialty. These include various white-collar classifications, such as social scientist or human resources, as well as various blue-collar classifications, such as electrical installation work or metal work. A detailed description of all the specific job titles that fall under each of these 59 categories is available in OPM's guide to data standards (OPM, undated [a]).

[2]   The numbers reflecting Hispanic representation across the labor forces differ slightly from those presented in Chapter Three because of different sample specifications. The CLF sample here drops federal workers (so that they are not in both comparison groups), keeps only full-time full-year workers (instead of all employed workers), and keeps non-U.S. citizens. The OPM data here drop almost 70,000 observations because they are missing information on at least one of the variables needed for analysis. In addition, the OPM data contain information on all federal workers. Hence, we do not weight these observations. When analyzing the CLF, we do use the sampling weights that the ACS provides.

[3]   Note that the federal government can employ non-U.S. citizens when there is no suitable applicant who is a U.S. citizen; this explains why the proportion of citizens in the federal workforce is not 100 percent.

[4]   *Metropolitan areas* here refers specifically to Core Based Statistical Areas (CBSAs). A CBSA is a geographic area that consists of one or more counties and an urban center of at least 10,000 people. In the ACS, data are aggregated to a higher geographic level (known as a Public Use Microdata Area), so we allowed ACS workers to be categorized as living in CBSAs if most people in their resident PUMAs were located in CBSAs.

Table 4.1
Individual and Occupation Characteristics in the Three Workforces

Variable	DoD Agencies (1)	CLF (2)	Non-DoD Federal Workforce (3)
Racial and ethnic group, as a percentage			
White	69.7	66.3	62.1
Black or African American	15.8	10.5	19.8
Hispanic	6.3	15.6	9.3
Asian, native Hawaiian, or other Pacific Islander	6.0	5.7	5.7
Other	2.2	2.0	3.1
Female, as a percentage	34.1	43.1	48.6
Employee age, in years	47.5	43.1	46.8
Years of educational attainment	14.6	13.8	15.0
U.S. citizen, as a percentage	100.0	91.3	99.9
Veteran, as a percentage	45.9	5.8	21.9
Occupational category, as a percentage			
Professional, white collar (P)	25.1	19.3	27.0
Administrative, white collar (A)	36.6	16.4	41.1
Technical, white collar (T)	14.5	9.6	18.1
Clerical, white collar (C)	3.9	18.3	5.3
Other, white collar (O)	3.4	5.3	4.4
Blue collar (B)	16.6	31.1	4.2
Resides in a metropolitan area, as a percentage	97.9	96.1	96.7
Federal job category, as a percentage			
Competitive service	93.0		69.3
Excepted service	6.8		30.1
SES general	0.1		0.3
SES career reserved	0.1		0.3
Sample	611,693	925,468	1,148,495

SOURCES: OPM and ACS data.

NOTE: For each variable in the table, all of the differences between columns (1) and (2) and between columns (1) and (3) are statistically significant at the $\alpha = 0.01$ level.

Characteristics of Hispanic and Non-Hispanic Workers

Overall, Table 4.1 shows significant differences among DoD, non-DoD federal, and all civilian workers. The relevant point for barrier analysis involves how the characteristics that are peculiar to DoD might affect the pool of potential Hispanic employees. For these differences to explain in part why Hispanics are underrepresented in DoD, Hispanic workers must be less likely to have the characteristics and job-specific skills that DoD agencies desire most. Table 4.2, listing comparative statistics for Hispanic and non-Hispanic workers in OPM and ACS data combined, suggests that this is the case.

Hispanic workers, on average, have lower education levels than non-Hispanic ones. They also tend to be younger, less likely to be U.S. citizens, less likely to be veter-

Table 4.2
Comparing Hispanic and Non-Hispanic Workers

Variable	Hispanics (1)	Non-Hispanics (2)
Female, as a percentage	38.2	44.0
Employee age, in years	39.4	43.9
Years of educational attainment	11.8	14.2
U.S. citizen, as a percentage	65.7	96.1
Veteran, as a percentage[a]	2.9	6.9
Occupational category, as a percentage		
Professional, white collar (P)	9.1	21.3
Administrative, white collar (A)	11.5	17.8
Technical, white collar (T)	8.1	10.1
Clerical, white collar (C)	16.9	18.2
Other, white collar (O)	3.5	5.6
Blue collar (B)	50.9	27.0
Resides in a metropolitan area, as a percentage	98.7	95.6
Federal job category (OPM only), as a percentage		
Competitive service	79.7	77.4
Excepted service	20.1	22.2
Sample	261,176	2,424,480

SOURCES: OPM and ACS data.

NOTE: For each variable in the table, all of the differences between columns (1) and (2) are statistically significant at the $\alpha = 0.01$ level.

[a] The percentage of all Hispanic workers in both populations who are veterans. An alternative reference point is that Hispanic representation in the full-time nonveteran CLF is 16.1 percent, compared with 7.1 percent in the veteran CLF.

ans, more likely to work in blue-collar jobs, and less likely to live in metropolitan areas. In each of these characteristics, Hispanic workers tend to be more similar to the CLF than to the DoD workforce, suggesting that these characteristics could pose barriers to Hispanic employment in DoD. We next calculate how much of the Hispanic representation gap can be attributed to these differences.

Blinder–Oaxaca Decomposition Results

One way to assess the relationship between each workforce's characteristics and the Hispanic representation gap is to ask the following question: If the DoD workforce characteristics (such as those in Table 4.1) were the same, on average, as those in the other workforce, how much would the gap narrow? If adjusting for these characteristics erases or erodes the gap, the gap might be related to workforce characteristics. If the gap were to remain or even increase after accounting for these characteristics, there are likely other causes for Hispanic underrepresentation in DoD.

We examine this question using the Blinder–Oaxaca decomposition method. This allows us to calculate how much of the representation gap is attributable to the net effect of all workforce characteristics, which is known as the explained component. The representation gap that remains after accounting for workforce characteristics (i.e., the difference between the original gap and the explained component) is known as the unexplained component. The results will inform DoD policymakers whether the gap is attributable to workforce structure and requirements or driven by other causes, such as differences in recruiting and outreach or potential discrimination.

The decomposition method can also determine how much each individual characteristic contributes to the explained component of the gap. This additional detail will inform policymakers about how individual characteristics influence the gap, potentially pointing to specific actions that DoD policymakers can take to make it an environment more conducive to hiring Hispanic employees. In online Appendix E, we discuss the specific calculations of the decomposition method analysis; below, we present the results and focus on the interpretation.

Comparing the Department of Defense Workforce and the Civilian Labor Force

Table 4.1 documented that 15.6 percent of the CLF is Hispanic, while only 6.3 percent of the DoD workforce is Hispanic. The difference between these two numbers, 9.3 percentage points, measures the gap in Hispanic representation across the two labor forces. The first two bars of Figure 4.1 depict the two workforce levels of Hispanic representation, as well as the representation gap. The third bar of Figure 4.1 displays the results of the decomposition analysis. The level of DoD representation is shown again, with additional sections that show how individual workforce characteristics affect the

Figure 4.1
Difference in Hispanic Representation Between the Department of Defense Workforce and the Civilian Labor Force, with Decomposition Results

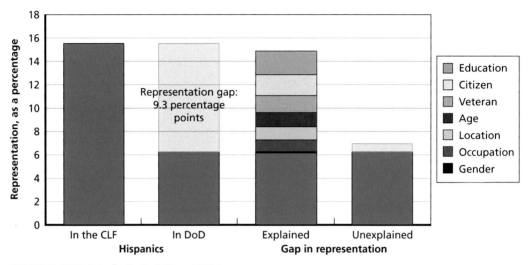

SOURCES: 2013 data for both ACS and OPM.
RAND RR1699-4.1

overall level of representation.[5] For example, the top section of the stacked bar has a height of approximately 2 percentage points, and it represents the effect of education. This bar indicates that 2 percentage points of the original gap in Hispanic representation can be attributed to different levels of education between the workforces. Alternatively, this result means that, if the two workforces had the same average education requirements, the gap would be 2 percentage points narrower (all else being equal).

Overall, Figure 4.1 shows that workforce characteristics explain most of the gap in representation between DoD and the CLF (about 92 percent). The fourth bar depicts the amount of the gap that remains after accounting for workforce characteristics (i.e., the unexplained component). The decomposition predicts that, if DoD and the CLF had the same average characteristics, the representation gap would shrink to less than 1 percentage point.

Table 4.3 summarizes these individual effects, with values identical to the heights of the corresponding sections of the stacked bar. The effects of the individual characteristics sum to the explained component, since they represent how much of the original gap is attributable to all characteristics. The remaining gap, or the unexplained component, represents the size of the gap that remains after workforce characteristics are taken into account.

---

[5]   The specific controls used include gender, age and its square, education level, U.S. citizenship status, veteran status, two-digit OPM occupational group, whether the worker was a resident of a CBSA, and state of residence.

Table 4.3
The Impact That Workforce Characteristics Have on the Gap in Hispanic Representation Between the Department of Defense Workforce and the Civilian Labor Force

Variable	Size of Effect on Hispanic Representation Gap Between Workforces, in Percentage Points
Total gap	9.3
Gender	0.03
Age	1.28
Education	2.05
U.S. citizen	1.80
Veteran status	1.38
Occupation	0.97
Location	1.11
Explained gap	8.62
Unexplained gap	0.72

SOURCES: OPM and ACS data.

NOTE: All values are statistically significant at the $\alpha = 0.001$ level. *Age* includes the combined impact of both age and its square; *education* includes the combined impact of all categories of educational attainment; *occupation* includes the combined impact of indicators for each of the 59 two-digit OPM occupation groups; and *location* includes the combined impact of state of residence and whether the person resided in a metropolitan area.

All characteristics except gender contribute meaningfully to the representation gap. Education and citizenship, each accounting for roughly 2 percentage points of the representation gap, play the largest role in explaining it. Although the education value listed in Table 4.3 includes the combined effect of adjusting for all education levels, more than two-thirds of the education effect arises from the high proportion of Hispanic workers in the CLF who do not have at least a high school diploma (or equivalent). The location portion of the explained component reflects the fact that DoD jobs are not geographically aligned with Hispanic workers in the CLF. For instance, 46 percent of Hispanic CLF workers live in either California or Texas, but these two states are home to only 16 percent of DoD employees (subsequent results examine the location effects in more detail). In the same way, the occupation portion of the explained component indicates that many Hispanics in the CLF work in occupations that are less common in DoD. Tables 4.1 and 4.2 hinted that this might be the case because they showed that more than half of Hispanic workers in our data were in blue-collar occupations but that these occupations were less common in DoD than in the CLF. Or to take a more precise example, 15 percent of Hispanic CLF workers are in occupations in the Food Preparation and Serving Family (7400), Plant and Animal Work Family (5000), or General Services and Support Work Family (3500). By contrast, less than 1 percent of DoD employees work in similar occupations. The decomposition value for occupation, then, essentially adjusts the representation level to account for the lack of DoD opportunities in occupation areas populated by Hispanic CLF workers.

Comparing the Department of Defense and Non–Department of Defense Federal Workforces

Table 4.1 indicates that the gap in Hispanic representation between DoD agencies, in which it is 6.3 percent, and the rest of the federal workforce, in which it is 9.3 percent, is 3 percentage points. The fact that this gap is smaller here than that between DoD and the CLF is to be expected; these labor forces are both within the federal system and have similarities that DoD does not share with the CLF. In particular, they have similar hiring practices, education requirements, and similar preferences for U.S. citizens and veterans. In this section, we determine how much of this gap can be explained by differences in characteristics between the two workforces.

Figure 4.2
Difference in Hispanic Representation Between the Department of Defense and the Non–Department of Defense Federal Workforces, with Decomposition Results

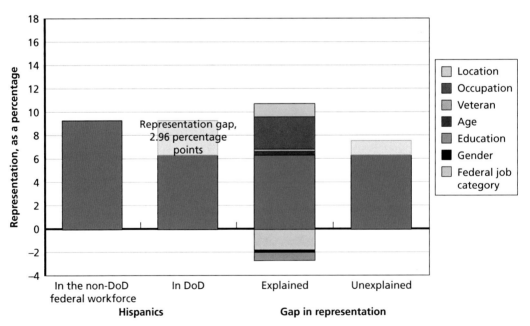

SOURCES: 2013 data for both ACS and OPM.
RAND RR1699-4.2

Figure 4.2 presents the overall results from the Blinder–Oaxaca decomposition. Similar to the previous comparison, the first two bars show the overall representation gap, and the third bar shows the results of the decomposition analysis. The workforce characteristics used in the decomposition include the same individual, location, and employment characteristics as in the DoD and CLF comparison except that (1) we do not control for citizenship, because it effectively does not vary within the federal workforce, and (2) we include federal job category here because it applies to all workers involved in this comparison.[6]

As in Figure 4.1, each stacked bar in Figure 4.2 represents the impact of the interworkforce differences in the characteristic on the representation gap. Unlike in Figure 4.1, some characteristics are represented below the 0-percent level on the horizontal axis, indicating that these characteristics have negative effects—that is, that a difference favors Hispanic representation in DoD. For example, the yellow section of the stacked bar representing the effect of federal job categories has a height of −1.8 percentage points. This result indicates that, if the workforces had the same average levels of competitive-service, excepted-service, and SES positions, the representation gap would be 1.8 percentage points larger.

Tables 4.1 and 4.2 shed light on the underlying dynamic behind this result. Specifically, Table 4.1 shows that a higher percentage of DoD workers are in competitive-service jobs, and Table 4.2 shows that Hispanic workers are slightly more likely than non-Hispanic workers to be in competitive-service jobs. Thus, the characteristic already favors DoD, so adjusting for it increases the gap.

The results in Figure 4.2 indicate that the net effect of all characteristics—subtracting the negative effects from the positive effects—accounts for nearly three-fifths of the initial 3-percent gap in representation, leaving an unexplained gap of 1.25 percentage points, as represented in orange on top of the fourth bar. That is, workforce characteristics can account for most of the representation gap between the DoD and non-DoD workforces, but there are still notable unexplained differences between them.

Table 4.4 lists the individual effects of the characteristics, as well as the values for the total gap, the explained gap, and the unexplained gap. In other words, these show the proportion of the gap that the characteristics account for, or the variance that can be attributed to the characteristics. All values correspond directly to the visual representation in Figure 4.2. The individual effects show that location and occupation differences between the two groups could more than account for the representation gap,[7]

---

[6] We did not use any of the other occupational controls that were available in the OPM data, such as whether the worker was in a supervisory position or the worker's GS level (if any). These variables highly overlap the detailed occupational control already being used, so a linear model cannot isolate their effect from the effect of occupation.

[7] Initially, the information in Tables 4.1 and 4.2 seems to suggest that occupation differences should favor DoD because a higher percentage of DoD jobs falls in the blue-collar category and because Hispanic workers have a

Table 4.4
The Impact That Workforce Characteristics Have on the Gap in Hispanic Representation Between the Department of Defense and Non–Department of Defense Federal Workforces

Variable	Size of Effect on Hispanic Representation Gap Between Workforces, in Percentage Points
Total gap	2.96
Gender	−0.19
Age	0.26
Education	−0.69
Veteran status	0.26
Occupation	2.73
Location	1.13
Federal job category	−1.78
Explained gap	1.71
Unexplained gap	1.25

SOURCES: OPM and ACS data.

NOTE: All values are statistically significant at the $\alpha = 0.001$ level. Negative values indicate that adjusting for the characteristic widens the Hispanic representation gap. The sum of the individual effects in the table does not exactly equal the explained gap because of rounding.

but these effects are offset by characteristics that are advantageous to DoD Hispanic representation. Additionally, although education explained part of the gap between DoD and the CLF, the education effect in this decomposition is negative, because non-DoD employees have slightly higher education levels than DoD employees.

Although we omitted the detailed decomposition of the *unexplained* component from the previous results for brevity, the unexplained effects of age and location indicate that these variables relate differently to representation in DoD and in the CLF. The following sections explore these relationships in more depth.

---

higher tendency to be in blue-collar jobs. In this comparison, we control for the two-digit OPM occupation group rather than the P, A, T, C, O, and B (PATCOB) categories (for more on PATCOB, see OPM, 2009). Hispanic members of the federal workforce are more likely to be in occupations that fall in the Inspection, Investigation, Enforcement, and Compliance Group (1800–1899), and these occupations are rare in DoD. Within this group, the occupation with the most Hispanic employees is the Border Patrol Enforcement series (1896).

Unexplained Patterns in Specific Workforce Characteristics

The previous results examined how altering the average characteristic levels affected the representation gap between DoD and the CLF or between the DoD and non-DoD federal workforces. However, another consideration for barrier analysis is that workforces could have similar average characteristics while having a barrier against a particular subset of the population. In this section, we examine two patterns beneath the surface of the previous results that point to potential areas for improvement in DoD Hispanic representation.

The first pattern involves differences in employee ages across populations. Table 4.3 indicates that differences in employee ages can explain 1.29 percentage points of the representation gap between DoD and the CLF, and Table 4.4 indicates that they can explain 0.26 percentage points of the representation gap between the DoD and non-DoD federal workforces. Age is also strongly related to the unexplained differences in Hispanic representation because Hispanic underrepresentation is more pronounced among younger workers for both DoD and non-DoD agencies. Figure 4.3 shows that Hispanic representation varies with age in the CLF, the non-DoD federal workforce, and the DoD workforce. Although the representation gap between DoD and the CLF is only 2 percentage points among workers at least 60 years of age, it is nearly 20 percentage points among workers less than 25 years of age.

Figure 4.3
Hispanic Representation, by Age Category, for the Civilian Labor Force, the Non–Department of Defense Federal Workforce, and the Department of Defense Workforce

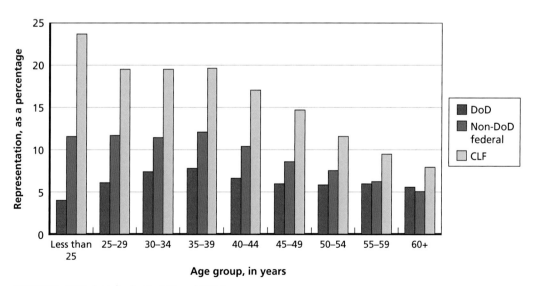

SOURCES: 2013 data for both ACS and OPM.

RAND RR1699-4.3

Thus, although age might function as a structural barrier to federal government work (perhaps the government requires more experience than the average CLF job, negatively affecting all younger workers, among whom Hispanic representation tends to be higher), this pattern indicates that this barrier is strongest among younger Hispanic workers. Such a barrier might be suitable for outreach efforts aimed at younger Hispanic workers in the CLF.

We also further investigated the relationship between Hispanic representation in the workforces and the geographic locations of workers. In the decomposition analysis, we included controls for workers' states of residence and whether they lived in metro areas, which captures the fact that DoD might offer fewer jobs in highly Hispanic states or in areas removed from cities. Individual state comparisons of representation also show that representation gaps are largest in states with the highest Hispanic populations. For example, although the overall representation gap between DoD and the CLF is 9.3 percentage points, the gap in California (the state with the largest Hispanic population) is 23.3 percentage points. This means that this barrier, like age, has multiple dimensions. There are fewer DoD workers in states with the largest Hispanic

Figure 4.4
Percentage of Hispanic Population and Department of Defense Workforce Located in Top Ten Hispanic Population Centers

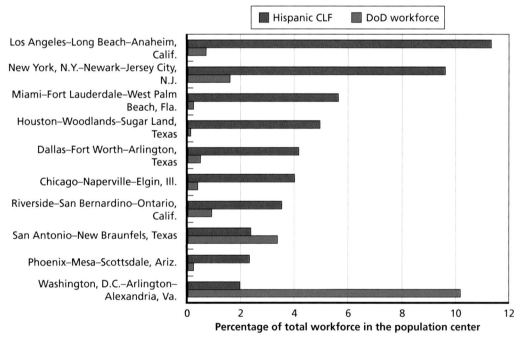

SOURCES: 2013 data for both ACS and OPM.

RAND RR1699-4.4

populations, but the representation gap between DoD workers and their fellow state residents is greater in highly Hispanic states.

One reason for this pattern could be that DoD job locations in highly Hispanic states do not align with Hispanic population centers. Figure 4.4 illustrates this problem, showing the ten metro areas with the highest Hispanic populations and, for each area, the percentage of all Hispanics in the CLF who reside there and the percentage of the DoD workforce located in that area.[8] These population centers contain nearly half the total Hispanic CLF but only 18 percent of the DoD workforce. Less than 3 percent of the DoD workforce is located in the Los Angeles, New York City, and Miami areas, which are home to more than 25 percent of the Hispanic CLF.

Figure 4.5 shows this geographic information for all CBSAs in the contiguous United States. This map illustrates the degree to which DoD locations overlap with the Hispanic CLF.

DoD locations do not generally overlap with Hispanic population centers. Other than the San Antonio area in central Texas and the San Diego area in southern California, Hispanic population centers tend to be distinct from DoD hubs. Hispanic workers in Miami, Chicago, or New York City are far removed from locations with many DoD employees. DoD hubs in northern and coastal Virginia, Oklahoma City, and the northern parts of Alabama and Utah are also far removed from Hispanic population centers.

Both the age and geography patterns are, by definition, unexplained by the decomposition analysis. However, they suggest potential areas for improvement. Even though average workforce characteristics can account for nearly the entire representation gap between DoD and the CLF, the results still point to problem areas among younger workers and in geographic areas with high Hispanic populations.

Summary

Our analysis of the DoD and CLF representation gap indicates that most general workforce characteristics tend to limit Hispanic representation in DoD and account for 92 percent of the observed representation gap. This means that the same relatively low level of Hispanic representation would be present in the CLF if all workers had to conform to DoD's unique structure.

More specifically, our analysis shows that the individual workforce characteristics of age, education, citizenship, veteran status, occupation type, and location each account for 1 to 2 percentage points of the overall representation gap. This indicates that there is no silver bullet for improving the representation gap. Each of these char-

---

[8] The top five locations with the largest DoD populations in 2013 were Washington–Arlington–Alexandria (10.2 percent), Virginia Beach–Norfolk–Newport News (6.3 percent), San Diego–Carlsbad (3.5 percent), San Antonio–New Braunfels (3.3 percent), and Baltimore–Columbia–Towson (3.2 percent).

Figure 4.5
Geographic Locations of Department of Defense Employees and the Full-Time Hispanic Civilian Labor Force, by Core Based Statistical Area

SOURCES: 2013 data for both ACS and OPM.
NOTE: The figure depicts full-time permanent DoD employees and Hispanic full-time workers in the CLF. We do not show relatively small populations in locations outside the continental United States (OCONUS). Orange stripes indicate full-time Hispanic workers; blue stripes indicate DoD workers. Areas with darker orange stripes have greater concentrations of Hispanic workers; those with darker blue stripes have greater concentrations of DoD workers.
RAND *RR1699-4.5*

acteristics has a separate impact even conditional on the others. For example, even if DoD were able to overcome the location effect with robust outreach and recruiting, the pipeline of new Hispanic recruits that such an effort would generate still faces the limitations of other requirements, such as citizenship and high school graduation. Thus, achieving a representative workforce might require targeted recruiting that is capable of significantly overrepresenting the eligible population of workers.

At the same time, the non-DoD federal workforce shares many of these barriers with DoD and yet has higher Hispanic representation even after accounting for characteristics. In particular, the non-DoD federal workforce appears to outperform DoD among younger employees. Although this analysis cannot explain the reasons for this pattern, it suggests that outreach among younger workers is a potential area for improvement. Additionally, the data show that the geography problem might be more complex than previously thought, in that DoD locations do not seem to align with Hispanic populations in areas where most potential recruits might live.

We cannot rule out the possibility that further unobservable labor market differences might contribute to the lower fraction of Hispanic employees in DoD than in the non-DoD federal workforce. It would be exceeding the limits of the methodology to suggest that the individual effects reported in Tables 4.3 and 4.4 indicate the predicted impact of changing any specific requirement. Policymakers might require a more detailed analysis with information on job requirements and applicants before determining that a requirement ought to be changed because it is a barrier to Hispanic applicants.

CHAPTER FIVE

Job-Applicant Data and Hispanic Representation in the Department of Defense

A missing link in our analysis so far is the one between the CLF and the DoD civilian workforce—namely, those people who apply for DoD jobs and engage in the federal hiring process. Knowledge of this population is a valuable component of barrier analysis because the composition of the applicant pool at various stages in the process indicates where the greatest reductions in Hispanic representation occur. Accurate applicant information allows better targeting of policies to minimize barriers to Hispanic representation.

Our analysis of job-applicant data sought to build on our findings that group differences in education, citizenship, age, location, and occupation could account for most of the Hispanic representation gap. For example, consider Hispanic CLF workers in occupations or fields that do not exist in DoD. Potential Hispanic applicants in these areas might not apply for DoD jobs at all (given that there are limited or no opportunities in their fields). Alternatively, they might apply for DoD jobs in similar fields but fail to make it past important hiring gates because they lack relevant experience. Each scenario would point to a different recommendation for addressing the barrier. Information on job applicants is the key to establishing the most appropriate course of action.

We used data on DoD job applicants captured through the federal government's official online job listing site, USAJOBS.gov. We compared this information with the most recent wave of DoD civilian workforce data. Our analyses suggest that Hispanic representation is higher among DoD applicants than among new DoD hires. This implies that Hispanic applicants are hired at lower rates than non-Hispanic ones. It is difficult, however, to establish whether Hispanic applicants are over- or underrepresented in the DoD applicant pool relative to the CLF because a large proportion of applicants do not provide race and ethnicity information. We found that barrier analysis results are sensitive to assumptions about applicants who do not provide demographic information on race and ethnicity.

We also examined whether job characteristics, such as occupation, grade, and location, are associated with whether the job received a Hispanic applicant. We found that the location of the job is the most important predictor of garnering a Hispanic applicant. We also found that Hispanic applicants' locations might be more closely related to the DoD presence in the area than to the Hispanic CLF population in that area. This suggests that the size of the Hispanic population near DoD installations influences Hispanic representation in the applicant pool.

Data on Online Department of Defense Job Applicants

We used applicant data from two sources. First, we obtained data on all DoD job applicants who applied through USAJOBS from 2012 to 2014. This information included demographic information from applicant profiles and was linked to corresponding job announcements. The USAJOBS data contain some applicant and job characteristics but no information on the results of the applications at any stage of the hiring process. The USAJOBS data on which we draw in the following section contained a total of about 1.8 million applicants with ethnicity information in 2014.

We also received USA Staffing AFD files for FY 2014. USA Staffing is an automated hiring software system that OPM provides to federal agencies. It builds from, but does not completely overlap with, the USAJOBS data. The AFD allow data on the hiring process to be captured, stripped of personally identifiable information, and used for assessment of the hiring process. The AFD contain fewer applicant characteristics than the USAJOBS data, but, unlike the USAJOBS data, the AFD have information on which applicants were determined to meet minimum qualifications (for certain applications), which were referred to selecting officials, and which were ultimately selected for positions. Including those with missing ethnicity information, the AFD contained 3.7 million applications, 1.1 million of which were referred and 91,342 of which were selected.

Some characteristics of the AFD limit our analyses. Although there is some information in the AFD on which applications met minimum qualifications, the data-capture process excludes certain applications, including those that were not referred to the review process and those that did not include demographic information.[1] To avoid the problems caused by excluded applications, our analysis of the AFD focused on the three major stages of the application process: application, referral, and selection. The AFD we used are at the application level (not the applicant level), with no means of identifying applicants who apply to more than one position. Large differences between ethnic groups in the number of applications could bias some calculations.[2] We also could not identify which applications were for full-time permanent

---

[1]   The AFD include a variable for the total number of applicants for each job, so we can determine how many applications did not provide demographic information. It is not, however, possible to determine which missing applications met minimum qualifications for the job.

[2]   Using the USAJOBS data, in which individual applicants can be identified, there did not appear to be large ethnic differences in the number of jobs for which applicants tended to apply, which suggests that this might not present a problem for our conclusions.

positions. Although previous chapters focused only on full-time permanent employees, our analysis of applicant data included all positions, including part-time and seasonal work. We did not expect this to greatly affect the results; 92 percent of the positions in DoD are full-time permanent positions.[3]

Because the USAJOBS data and the AFD provide different types of information on job applicants and have different limitations, we attempted to draw on both sources for inferences about the application process. As in previous chapters, we compared these data with the OPM civilian personnel data files. The most recent year available for the OPM data files is 2013.

Hispanic Representation Through the Department of Defense Application Process

The EEOC benchmark for 2013 indicates that 11 percent of the CLF was Hispanic in 2013, whereas 6 percent of DoD employees were.[4] We sought to determine whether the low level of Hispanic representation in DoD stems from a shortage of Hispanic applicants or from a low number of Hispanic applicants completing the various stages of the application process.

Because 57 percent of applications do not include ethnicity information (see Figure 5.1, right panel), we could not determine whether they are Hispanic. As Figure 5.1 indicates, self-identified Hispanics complete 19 percent of applications providing ethnicity information but only 8 percent of all applications. If applications without ethnicity information are less likely to be from Hispanic applicants, excluding them would cause overestimation of Hispanic representation at each stage in the process. If such applications are disproportionately selected, Hispanic underrepresentation among selectees could be hidden by excluding the applications without ethnicity information in the barrier analysis.

Given the uncertainty over the composition of the missing applications, we calculated a plausible range of values for representation at each phase of the process. The upper bound of this range is the Hispanic representation at a given stage under the assumption that Hispanic and non-Hispanic applicants are equally likely to provide demographic information.[5] Essentially, the upper bound is the level of Hispanic rep-

---

[3] Later analysis, using USAJOBS data rather than the AFD, will also show that Hispanic applicants do not appear more likely to apply for intermittent or part-time work, conditional on other factors.

[4] In this instance, *the CLF* refers to the population that is 16 years of age or older who were employed or seeking employment, excluding the armed forces and noncitizens.

[5] The missing applicants might also be *more* likely to be Hispanic, and the true representation might be much higher than this upper bound. Nevertheless, comparing the CLF and OPM data suggests that applicants without identifying data are disproportionately non-Hispanic—making it unlikely that missing-data applicants are *more* likely to be Hispanic.

Figure 5.1
Hispanic Representation Among All Fiscal Year 2014 Department of Defense Applications

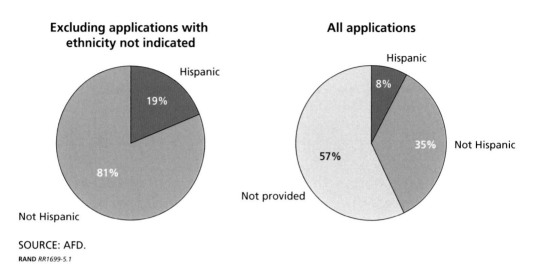

SOURCE: AFD.
RAND *RR1699-5.1*

resentation among only applications with demographic information. This is likely the approach that analysts take when using AFD for barrier analysis. The lower bound of our range is the value of Hispanic representation assuming that all missing applications are from non-Hispanic applicants. Figure 5.2 presents the plausible ranges of Hispanic applications at each phase in the process, as well as benchmarks denoting Hispanic representation in the CLF, among new DoD hires, and among all DoD civilian employees.

When comparing Hispanic representation in the AFD with representation in the CLF and in the OPM data, it appears that the true representation level for DoD at each stage is probably closer to the lower bounds shown. If 19 percent of the DoD applicant pool and 16 percent of the selected DoD applicants were actually Hispanic, it would be difficult to explain the low levels of representation among new hires found in the OPM data, in which race and ethnicity information is almost universally known.[6] Assuming that most or all DoD applicants who do not provide ethnicity information are not Hispanic, we conclude that representation in the DoD applicant pool is likely between the level in the CLF and the level among DoD civilian employees. Hispanic DoD applications appear to have qualifications that are generally similar to non-Hispanic DoD applicants on average: Hispanic representation among referred applications is similar to that among all applications. Still, although at least 8 percent of referred DoD applications are from Hispanics, only 6 percent of applications selected are Hispanic—

---

[6] Hispanic selectees could be less likely to accept job offers from DoD, or they could be less likely to navigate onboarding requirements, such as background investigations. Additionally, Hispanic applicants could have a tendency to change their ethnic identification after being hired. Each of these explanations seems less likely than the possibility that non-Hispanic applicants are less likely to provide ethnicity information.

Figure 5.2
Hispanic Representation, by Application Stage, with Civilian Labor Force and Department of Defense Employee Benchmarks, 2013 and 2014

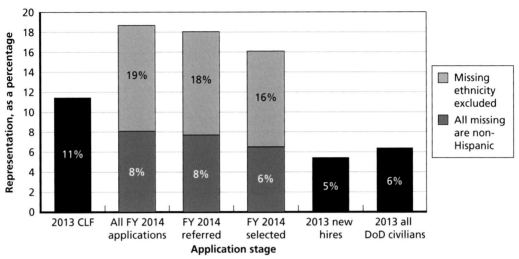

SOURCES: ACS data, AFD, and OPM data. Application data are from FY 2014 (October 1, 2013, through September 30, 2014), while data on DoD civilians are drawn from a 2013 snapshot.
NOTE: In this chapter, we had to use different years for application data and hiring data because access to employee data was limited to only 2008 through 2013 and to application data to only FY 2014 and FY 2015. This means that new employees in this figure are not drawn from the applicant pool in the figure. This limits our ability to describe applicant behavior. If there is significant annual variation in hiring for agency–job series pairs, the conclusions we based on these data might be wrong. Because there is so little variation in the proportion of Hispanics among new hires in the five years for which we have new-hire data, however, we consider it very unlikely that the gap we found in Hispanic representation in selected applications and new hires is an artifact of our data. Between 2009 and 2013, Hispanics made up about 5 percent to 6 percent of new hires each year. In the 2014 applicant data, Hispanics made up about 7 percent of selected applicants. The proportion of Hispanics among new hires in 2014 would have to increase about one-fifth from the previous year's level for there to be no gap in their representation among selected applications and new hires.
RAND RR1699-5.2

which is similar to the levels of representation seen in the 2013 OPM data for new hires and all employees.

Figure 5.3 illustrates this somewhat differently, showing the ethnicity-specific rates of referral and selection (among applications that were referred). We calculated these rates by excluding DoD applications with missing ethnicity. This does not affect the rate comparisons in the same way as it affects representation because there was virtually no difference between the missing applications and the non-Hispanic DoD applications in the observed referral and selection rates. The differences depicted in Figure 5.3 are too small to be considered practically significant if an 80-percent rule of thumb is applied, but, given the large number of applications, they are statistically

Figure 5.3
Department of Defense Referral and Selection Rates, by Ethnicity, in Fiscal Year 2014

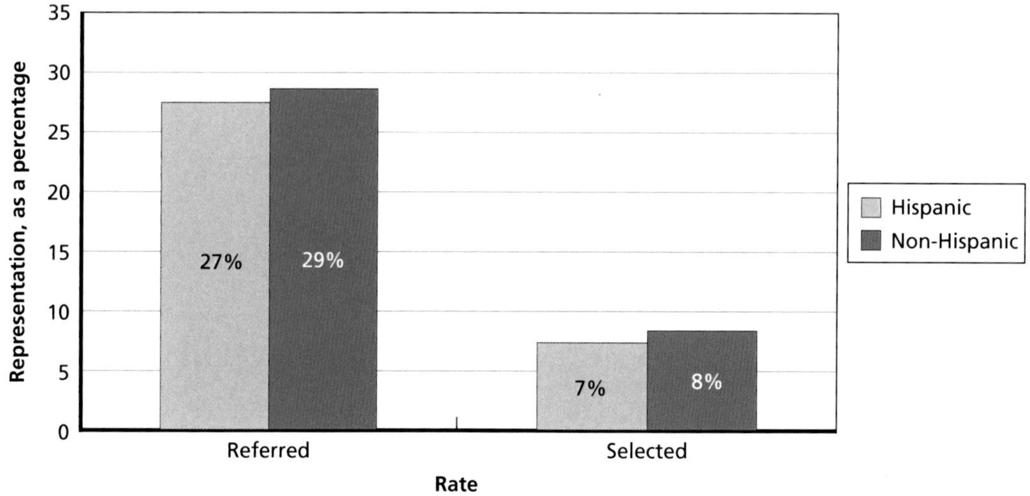

SOURCE: AFD.
NOTE: Both differences between Hispanic and non-Hispanic applications are statistically significant.
RAND RR1699-3.5

significant.[7] It appears that Hispanic DoD applications are referred and selected at slightly lower rates than non-Hispanic DoD applications.[8]

Possible Reasons for Ethnic Differences in Propensity to Provide Demographic Information

Although the AFD point to potential systematic underreporting of demographic information among non-Hispanic applicants, this pattern would be somewhat unusual. Typically, government agencies are concerned that minority groups have a lower likelihood of survey inclusion, although this is not the same thing as declining to answer a survey question (U.S. Bureau of Labor Statistics and U.S. Census Bureau, 2002). Other research has shown no difference between highly Hispanic areas and highly

---

[7]   Compared with the analyses in Chapter Three, the analyses in this chapter and in online Appendix C are more aligned with the traditional application of adverse-impact analyses. Online Appendix D provides analyses addressing job positions within each agency. Where discrepancies exist, additional adverse-impact analyses could also consider the validity of selection procedures for positions.

[8]   We considered two possibilities that could explain the lower referral and selection rates by examining the types of jobs receiving applications. First, Hispanics might be more likely to apply to more-competitive jobs. Second, because not all jobs appear on USAJOBS and because some jobs are omitted from the OPM data files (because of sensitivity), there might be a spurious difference in selection of Hispanic applications. We used job series and agency information to compare application data with those on new hires and determined that neither of these possibilities is a likely explanation for the decreased representation at the selection stage.

white (non-Hispanic) areas in reasons for declining to respond to surveys (Griffin, 2002).[9]

It is difficult to be sure why many applicants do not provide demographic information in the AFD. Any conclusions or results from the analysis of these data sets should be viewed with caution, and OPM should review the process of collecting and capturing race and ethnicity information from applicants and improve response rates before making policy decisions based on applicant data.

Hispanic Versus Non-Hispanic Department of Defense Applicant Qualifications

To further investigate whether Hispanic and non-Hispanic DoD applicants have similar qualifications, we can draw on the USAJOBS data from FY 2014. This includes general self-reported qualifications that can be found in an applicant's profile. The USAJOBS data had far fewer missing values for demographics, possibly because they are captured at a different point in the application process.[10] Table 5.1 shows education, experience, and citizenship information for Hispanic and non-Hispanic DoD applicants to jobs that closed out in FY 2014.[11] The table suggests that Hispanic and non-Hispanic DoD applicants might have very similar qualifications, broadly speaking, although these categories are far more general than the information that would be available to selecting officials.

There was no difference in citizenship status between Hispanic and non-Hispanic DoD applicants. More than 99 percent of applicants from both groups reported being U.S. citizens. Reported educational attainment was very similar for Hispanic and non-Hispanic applicants. Regarding career experience, Hispanic applicants were more likely to be students and less likely to be in the more-experienced categories (entry level through subject-matter expert), but the differences with non-Hispanic applicants were small. Hispanic applicants were about as likely as non-Hispanics to be current or former federal employees, suggesting that non-Hispanics did not enjoy an insider

---

[9]   If nonresponse were resulting from strategic behavior among applicants who fear that their ethnicity will negatively affect their likelihood of obtaining a job, it could lead to underreporting among Hispanic applicants rather than white applicants, given previous evidence of Hispanic disadvantages in the civilian labor market (Kenney and Wissoker, 1994). Alternatively, a widespread perception that being Hispanic is an advantage in the application process could theoretically create the observed pattern of nonresponse, but we know of no research documenting such a pattern in practice.

[10]   In conversations with subject-matter experts, it became apparent that an applicant can include demographic information in the standing profile without transmitting the information when submitting an application. The additional information in the USAJOBS data could be from the individual profiles and not from the submitted applications. This discrepancy also highlights the need for consistent and accurate data collection.

[11]   Education information was missing for approximately 40 percent of the job applicants because information was available only for applicants who built their resumes through the USAJOBS resume builder. There were only small differences by ethnicity in the availability of education level, so this should not greatly affect the comparison in Table 5.1.

Table 5.1
Percentage of Hispanic and Non-Hispanic Department of Defense Applicants in Each Education, Experience, and Citizenship Category in Fiscal Year 2014

Characteristic	Hispanic	Non-Hispanic
Educational attainment		
Less than high school	0.4	0.5
High school or equivalent	15.2	16.2
Some college	21.7	20.1
Associate's degree	7.0	6.9
Bachelor's degree	29.3	28.6
Master's degree	19.8	20.9
Professional degree	4.4	4.5
Doctorate degree	2.1	2.4
Citizenship		
U.S. citizen	99.2	99.4
Highest level of career experience		
High school student	6.1	5.8
College student	17.8	14.9
Graduate or postgraduate student	9.6	8.1
Entry level	9.0	9.6
Midcareer	26.3	27.8
Manager	23.5	24.5
Executive	3.2	3.9
Senior executive	0.8	1.1
Subject-matter expert	3.7	4.2
Federal employment status		
Current federal employee	25.5	25.7
Former federal employee	8.8	8.6
Never a federal employee	65.8	65.7
Veteran status		
Veteran	35.6	33.6

SOURCE: USAJOBS data.

NOTE: Differences between Hispanic and non-Hispanic patterns in each category are statistically significant.

advantage. Finally, Hispanic applicants were slightly more likely to be veterans than non-Hispanic applicants were.

Altogether, these data suggest that Hispanic representation in the applicant pool is probably higher than it is among new DoD hires but lower than what it is in the CLF. This is consistent with our earlier analysis regarding structural barriers in DoD employment. The data also suggest that Hispanic DoD applicants have qualifications similar to those of non-Hispanic applicants. This is evident in levels of self-reported education and experience, as well as in similar levels of referral for Hispanics and non-Hispanics.

Department of Defense Job Characteristics That Increase the Likelihood of a Hispanic Applicant

To determine which job characteristics affect whether a DoD job will receive a Hispanic applicant, we use the variation in the job characteristics of advertised positions in 2014. We draw on the USAJOBS data rather than the AFD because the USAJOBS data included more-detailed job characteristics, such as possible locations for the work.

Our earlier analysis suggested that Hispanic representation is lower in DoD than in the CLF in part because Hispanics tend to be younger and less educated than DoD workers. The average Hispanic CLF worker is also more likely to live away from DoD employment hubs and to work in occupations with fewer DoD opportunities. The USAJOBS data can offer further insights here. In particular, if these characteristics are barriers to Hispanic employment in DoD, jobs with these characteristics should be less likely to receive Hispanic applicants.

Methodology: Logistic Regression

We seek to understand whether particular characteristics are associated with the likelihood that a given DoD job received a Hispanic applicant, conditional on other available characteristics. The outcome variable—whether a DoD job received a Hispanic applicant—is dichotomous. This makes logistic regression an appropriate tool to assess the relationship between the job characteristics and the probability of a Hispanic applicant. This method assumes that there is an additive relationship between all potential characteristics and the likelihood of a Hispanic applicant. It then uses the observed patterns in the data to infer the strength of the association between each characteristic and the outcome. The advantage of this approach over simple summary statistics is that it enables us to examine the partial effect of each variable, conditional on the other characteristics.

The subsequent results present the average marginal effect that each variable has on the probability of a Hispanic DoD applicant. These values can be interpreted as the average change in the probability of a Hispanic DoD applicant associated with a small change in the predictor, holding all other values constant. For the categorical variables, the average marginal effect is the average change in probability associated with a given characteristic, relative to the base category.

Table 5.2 lists all job characteristics that we included in the model as potential predictors of whether a DoD job applicant was Hispanic. The analysis included 124,066 DoD job announcements, 13 percent of which received Hispanic applicants.

Results

The largest differences in the probability that a position received a Hispanic applicant were related to the potential locations listed in the job announcement. Figure 5.4 shows the average marginal effect for each location that was significantly more likely to receive a Hispanic applicant.

Jobs that listed locations in New Mexico, for instance, were 15 percentage points more likely than jobs that did not have openings in New Mexico to receive Hispanic applicants. Most other locations shown in Figure 5.4 are also Hispanic population centers, with New Jersey also being adjacent to a large Hispanic population in the New York City metro area. The greater likelihood that OCONUS jobs received Hispanic applicants than jobs elsewhere is attributable to several jobs advertising locations in Puerto Rico.

Table 5.3 shows the average marginal effects for the characteristics other than location, along with their standard errors. It shows some statistically significant relationships, but none of these characteristics affects the probability of a Hispanic applicant by more than 3 percentage points. In other words, these effects are all less than those shown for each location indicated in Figure 5.4.

The lack of a statistically significant difference between blue-collar and professional white-collar jobs appears to indicate that DoD blue-collar jobs are not more likely to receive Hispanic applicants, but this result is due to the model structure,

Table 5.2
Potential Predictors of Whether a Department of Defense Job Received a Hispanic Applicant

Characteristic	Description
Location	State listed on job announcement as a potential location
Occupation	PATCOB classification of advertised occupation
Grade	Minimum grade level (e.g., "11" for a job advertised as "GS-11 to GS-13")
Supervisory	Whether the job was listed as a supervisory position
Work schedule	Advertised schedule (full time, part time, or other)
Work type	Type of work (e.g., permanent, temporary, seasonal)
Pay schedule	Whether the job listed was for GS, wage grade, or other
Department	Whether the job listed was under DoD or Department of the Air Force, Army, or Navy

Figure 5.4
Positive and Significant Average Marginal Effects for Department of Defense Job Locations from Logistic Regression Predicting the Probability of a Hispanic Applicant

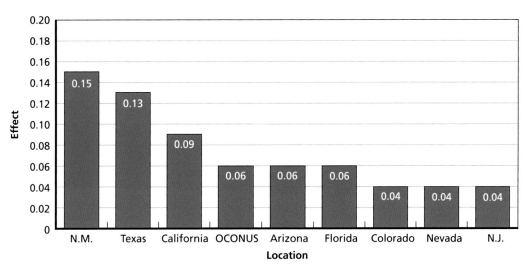

SOURCE: USAJOBS data for positions that opened in 2014.
NOTE: All values are statistically significant at the 0.05 level. Some advertisements listed multiple locations, so each location's marginal effect can be interpreted relative to all jobs that did not advertise positions for that location. These effects are conditional on other controls listed in Table 5.2.
RAND RR1699-5.4

which included the job's pay plan. DoD jobs that were on wage-grade pay plans, which include the vast majority of blue-collar jobs, were about 2 percentage points more likely to receive Hispanic applicants than other pay plans. Jobs on GS pay plans were also more likely to receive Hispanic applicants than other pay plans, but this difference is smaller than the difference for wage-grade jobs. Our model thus suggests that Hispanic applicants are more likely to apply for blue-collar jobs but not for blue-collar jobs from pay plans other than wage grade.

There is also some evidence that Hispanic DoD applicants might be more interested in work requiring less education or experience. This might be related to the fact that the Hispanic population tends to be younger and less educated than the non-Hispanic population. Administrative white-collar and clerical white-collar jobs were more likely than professional white-collar jobs to receive Hispanic applicants, which could be partly attributable to lower education requirements in these areas. Certain occupational codes specifically designate whether a job is for a trainee in any area, and all trainee jobs are classified in the other white-collar occupation category. The fact that jobs in the other white-collar occupation category had the highest likelihood of receiving Hispanic applicants also reflects a potential Hispanic preference for entry-level work appropriate for a younger population. Increasing pay grade was associated with a decreasing likelihood of a Hispanic DoD applicant.

Table 5.3
Average Marginal Effects from Logistic Regression Predicting the Probability of a Hispanic Department of Defense Applicant

Characteristic	Marginal Effect	Standard Error
Occupation (base: professional, white collar)		
Administrative, white collar	0.013***	0.003
Technical, white collar	0.007	0.004
Clerical, white collar	0.016***	0.004
Other, white collar	0.022**	0.007
Blue collar	0.006	0.007
Supervisory level	−0.004	0.003
Department (base: DoD)		
Air Force	−0.012**	0.004
Army	−0.0002	0.004
Navy	−0.021***	0.004
Pay series (base: other)		
GS	0.01*	0.005
Wage grade	0.019*	0.008
Lower grade limit	−0.003***	<0.001
Work type (base: permanent)		
Temporary or term	0.003	0.003
Multiple types	−0.016***	0.005
Seasonal or intermittent	0.004	0.008
Intern or recent graduate	−0.013	0.007
Other	−0.003	0.005
Work schedule (base: full time)		
Part time	0.005	0.007
Multiple or other	0.012	0.006

SOURCE: USAJOBS data for positions that opened in 2014.

NOTE: *, **, and *** denote statistical significance at the 0.05, 0.01, and 0.001 levels, respectively. Our model also included indicator variables for each state and for OCONUS locations listed on the job announcement. We included a polynomial term for lower grade limit. The model had a pseudo R-squared value of 0.037, suggesting that it was able to explain only a limited amount of variation in the outcome.

Other patterns are less consistent with this idea. Positions for recent graduates and interns were not significantly different from permanent positions in the likelihood of receiving Hispanic applicants. Hispanic applicants were also no less likely to apply to supervisory positions than nonsupervisory positions, all else being equal.

Further Detail on the Locations of Department of Defense Job Applicants Versus Department of Defense Employees

A key result of the regression analysis is that job location appears to play a strong role in determining which jobs receive Hispanic applicants. Previous chapters noted that DoD job locations do not generally overlap with Hispanic population centers, even within highly Hispanic states. This lack of overlap could explain the relative under-representation of Hispanic employees. We use USAJOBS data to explore the most-common locations from which recent Hispanic applicants for DoD jobs originated.

In Chapter Four, we showed that many Hispanic population centers were geographically separated from locations that are large hubs for DoD workers. For example, Hispanic CLF workers in Chicago, Miami, and New York City are geographically removed from the large concentration of DoD workers in Virginia, the District of Columbia, and Maryland. One question that the USAJOBS data might answer is whether DoD is still able to draw Hispanic applicants from these areas or whether Hispanic applicants are more likely to come from locations that are closer to DoD hubs.

To investigate this question, Figures 5.5 and 5.6 show two maps. The first map depicts the relative locations of all DoD employees and Hispanic CLF workers. The CBSAs with more DoD employees have darker blue stripes, while the CBSAs with more Hispanic CLF employees have darker orange stripes. The second map uses color intensity to indicate how many Hispanic applicants originated from the area in 2013. Comparing the second map to the first shows where Hispanic applicants originate and whether those areas are correlated with the number of DoD or Hispanic CLF workers.

The contrast between California and Texas is instructive. In California, Hispanic DoD applicants tended to originate from both the San Diego area, which has a high concentration of DoD employees, and from the Los Angeles area, which has many Hispanic CLF workers and far fewer DoD employees. In Texas, by contrast, Hispanic DoD applicants originated almost exclusively from the DoD hub of San Antonio, whereas very few applicants arose from the high concentrations of Hispanic workers in Houston and Dallas–Fort Worth. These results suggest potential areas of improvement for DoD. In Texas, Hispanic applicants tended to originate from the location where DoD employees already have a large presence, but California demonstrates that it might be possible to attract Hispanic applicants from nearby population centers with relatively few DoD jobs.

Figure 5.5
Department of Defense and Hispanic Civilian Labor-Force Worker Locations from 2013 Office of Personnel Management and American Community Survey Data, with Greater Color Intensity for Areas with More Workers of That Type

SOURCES: 2013 OPM, ACS, and USAJOBS data.
NOTE: The figure shows DoD and Hispanic CLF worker locations with varying intensity according to how many Hispanic applicants originated from the location. DoD workers are in blue, and Hispanic CLF workers are in orange. Areas with larger Hispanic CLF populations are shown in darker orange, while areas with larger DoD populations are shown in darker blue. We do not show the relatively small populations in OCONUS locations. The map varies the color intensity according to how many Hispanic applicants originated from each area. For California and Texas, we calculated applicant intensity at the CBSA level. For all other locations, we calculated it at the state level. This is because the USAJOBS data do not have CBSA information. We coded CBSAs from city name strings for Texas and California, but developing CBSA-level information for all locations was not feasible.
RAND *RR1699-5.5*

Virginia stands out in the second map, suggesting that many Hispanic applicants originated from the vicinity of the DoD concentration in Washington, D.C. In this case, the large number of Hispanic DoD applicants likely results from more job opportunities in the area. Still, Figures 5.5 and 5.6 suggest that some applicants originate from states with relatively few DoD employees nearby: Florida and New York retain some brightness in the second map. At the same time, relatively few Hispanic applicants came from other geographically separated Hispanic areas, such as the Chicago metro area.

Overall, our results support our hypothesis that DoD attracts applicants from areas close to its existing locations but that those locations do not align well with His-

Figure 5.6
Department of Defense and Hispanic Civilian Labor-Force Worker Locations, with Greater Intensity for High Hispanic Department of Defense Applicant Areas

Hispanic applicants tend to originate from locations with high DoD presence

Relatively few Hispanic applicants originate from key Hispanic population centers

SOURCES: 2013 OPM, ACS, and USAJOBS data.
NOTE: The figure shows DoD and Hispanic CLF worker locations with varying intensity according to how many Hispanic applicants originated from the location. DoD workers are in blue, and Hispanic CLF workers are in orange. Areas with larger Hispanic CLF populations are shown in darker orange, while areas with larger DoD populations are shown in darker blue. We do not show the relatively small populations in OCONUS locations. This map varies the color intensity according to how many Hispanic applicants originated from each area. For California and Texas, we calculated applicant intensity at the CBSA level. For all other locations, we calculated it at the state level. This is because the USAJOBS data do not have CBSA information. We coded CBSAs from city name strings for Texas and California, but developing CBSA-level information for all locations was not feasible.
RAND RR1699-5.6

panic population centers. At the same time, these results show that this geographic barrier can be overcome for at least some Hispanic applicants, suggesting that increased recruiting and outreach efforts can further reduce this barrier.

Summary

Our findings indicate that Hispanic representation in the applicant pool, like that among all DoD employees, is likely lower than the CLF benchmark. We cannot be confident in this conclusion, however, because a large proportion of the AFD does not have ethnicity information. Through the DoD application process, Hispanic applicants have slightly lower referral and selection rates than non-Hispanic applicants, suggesting that representation in the Hispanic population who are selected for DoD jobs slightly lags behind representation in the applicant pool. Hispanic and non-Hispanic applicants appeared to have similar characteristics, although Hispanic applicants tend to have lower levels of career experience.

Our analysis of the application process also highlights the importance of understanding how and when applicant data are captured and how to consider applicants with missing demographic information. Different assumptions about applications with missing demographic information led to vastly different conclusions in barrier analysis. We recommend analyzing ethnicity-specific rates of referral and selection, rather than representation in the referred and selected populations, because this technique was much more robust to different assumptions about the missing data.

Job location appears to most influence whether a job will receive Hispanic applicants. Hispanic applicants also appear to be more likely to seek blue-collar jobs or jobs at lower pay grades that are appropriate for younger or less educated workers.

Hispanic applicants to DoD are more likely to come from areas with a large DoD presence. This suggests that, even within states with significant Hispanic populations, the location of DoD installations can affect Hispanic representation in the workforce. The fact that key DoD hubs are not located in Hispanic population centers presents an additional challenge to reducing barriers to Hispanic employment and underscores the importance of outreach and recruiting in meeting representation goals.

All these analyses demonstrate a need to improve job-applicant data collection. Given that much of the gap in Hispanic DoD representation appears to be explainable, DoD recruiting efforts aiming to overcome these barriers to Hispanic employment depend on having accurate information about applicants and their characteristics. Job-applicant data, however, are of limited quality and detail, which limits how well recruiting policies can be targeted.

CHAPTER SIX

Qualitative Assessment of Hispanic Representation Gaps in the Department of Defense Civilian Workforce: Representative Department of Defense Perspectives

To complement our quantitative analyses and provide additional insights into Hispanic underrepresentation in the DoD civilian workforce, we interviewed DoD personnel and representatives of HSIs on their perceptions of barriers regarding employment of Hispanics, as well as relevant DoD policies, procedures, and practices. This chapter discusses findings from DoD personnel; Chapter Seven discusses findings from representatives of HSIs.

Overview of Qualitative Analysis and Methodology

We conducted 19 semistructured interviews with DoD personnel. We conducted these interviews with EEO and diversity staff, as well as hiring managers and supervisors, including representatives from each of the military services (i.e., Air Force, Army, and Navy) and some DoD agencies (e.g., DLA, Defense Commissary Agency, Washington Headquarters Services). Interviews with EEO and diversity personnel at the headquarters level provided perspectives of those whose primary mission involves understanding representation of demographic groups within the DoD workforce. They provided input on perceived barriers to increased Hispanic representation, as well as the relevant policies and practices that can affect Hispanic representation. DoD hiring managers and supervisors provided input on how those policies and practices are implemented, as well as additional perspectives on potential barriers to Hispanic representation from those whose mission is broader than promoting EEO and diversity. Interviewees from DoD's Recruitment Assistance Division (RAD), which leads DoD's marketing efforts for civilian employment opportunities, provided perspectives on DoD outreach and recruitment initiatives for civilian careers (Defense Civilian Personnel Advisory Service [DCPAS], undated [a]). We identified DoD interview participants primarily through snowball sampling, beginning with key diversity and EEO personnel from each military service.[1]

---

[1] *Snowball sampling* is a sampling technique by which initial study participants identify and suggest additional study participants to the research team.

Our interviews with DoD personnel were approximately one hour in length and were conducted by phone and in person. We asked participants about perceptions of barriers and reasons for them, as well as outreach and recruitment, hiring, retention, and promotion strategies relevant to Hispanic workers. The topics we discuss in more depth emerged from our interviews; we did not ask about specific practices or programs. See online Appendix F for the full interview protocol. We coded our interview notes for content and analyzed them to identify key themes and trends. We also reviewed supporting documents that interview participants provided.

Qualitative Assessment Findings

We summarize findings from our DoD interviews by topic area: potential barriers to Hispanic representation, outreach and recruiting strategies, hiring strategies, and promotion and retention strategies. We also highlight two promising practices within the department that emerged from our interviews.

Structural, Psychological, and Behavioral Barriers

Nearly all DoD interviewees reported experiences consistent with our data suggesting lower participation rates for Hispanics than others in the DoD civilian workforce. They noted both structural barriers and potential behavioral or psychological barriers as possible explanations for the trend.

Structural barriers they noted included the geographic location of DoD civilian jobs available, with nearly half of DoD interviewees mentioning this issue. Many interviewees perceived that DoD jobs are not in areas of high Hispanic populations and that Hispanics were often not interested in moving outside their communities to DoD jobs. For example, one interviewee noted that, when her organization has vacancies in areas with large numbers of Hispanics, they can often fill the position with a Hispanic applicant, but finding Hispanic applicants in other areas can be a challenge.

Another structural barrier mentioned as potentially contributing to Hispanic underrepresentation was emphasis given to veterans' preference in the DoD hiring process, according to just over one-quarter of DoD interviewees. Some interviewees noted that veteran candidates push out nonveteran candidates for DoD positions—and that Hispanics are less represented among veterans than non-Hispanics are.

Interviewees also noted several potential behavioral or psychological contributors to Hispanic underrepresentation in the DoD civilian workforce. Nearly one-third of interviewees mentioned a perception within DoD of citizenship or language barriers among Hispanics. Some interviewees also thought that Hispanics might be deterred from applying to DoD positions because of English language requirements or citizenship requirements and related security clearance requirements. Even if a potential applicant is a U.S. citizen, some interviewees noted, the potential applicant might have parents or other family members who are not U.S. citizens or even in the country illegally and fear repercussions from pursuing DoD employment.

Close to one-third of interviewees said that there might be a lack of awareness regarding Hispanic underrepresentation within DoD and a lack of motivation to address the issue. Many interviewees felt that messaging on the importance of the issue from DoD senior leaders is lacking. They also noted that hiring managers needed to be made aware of Hispanic underrepresentation and educated on how to address it. About 16 percent of interviewees also suggested attitudinal barriers as a possible contributor to Hispanic underrepresentation. For example, one interviewee said that some hiring managers might have an unconscious bias and be deterred from hiring a Hispanic candidate with an accent.

A few interviewees, 10 percent, noted the challenges of building a community within their organizations that is welcoming to Hispanic employees and includes a strong network of existing Hispanic employees. This lack of community was seen as potentially making recruiting and retaining Hispanic employees more difficult. Some interviewees felt that an organization that already has a community of Hispanic employees would be more likely to attract additional Hispanic employees.

Overall, the most–frequently mentioned barriers were

- geographic location of DoD civilian positions
- citizenship or language requirements for DoD employment
- lack of awareness and motivation from leaders and managers to address Hispanic underrepresentation.

In the next section, we consider possible strategies that interviewees suggested to overcome these barriers.

Outreach and Recruiting

Our interviews found that the level of effort supporting Hispanic outreach and recruitment varied greatly by military service and agency. Some interviewees reported that their organizations had no targeted efforts to recruit Hispanics, while others mentioned ongoing initiatives. Many said that, overall, DoD was not doing enough targeted outreach to the Hispanic community, specifically for civilian opportunities. Interviewees often cited funding constraints on targeted outreach efforts.

DoD's RAD oversees DoD civilian recruiting efforts. It focuses outreach on a broad overview of DoD civilian opportunities rather than filling specific positions. RAD facilitates a DoD Recruiters' Consortium to provide a forum for outreach collaboration across the department and promote an overarching branding of DoD civilian careers. It does not focus specifically on recruitment of Hispanic civilians.

About half of our DoD interviewees noted at least one of two current outreach and recruiting strategies that they felt could be leveraged to a greater extent within their organizations and across DoD. One is targeted recruitment in geographic areas with large Hispanic populations, as well as at HSIs. This targeted recruitment aims to increase awareness of DoD civilian opportunities within the Hispanic community and increase the number of Hispanic applicants. The other is partnerships with Hispanic organizations, such as the Society of Hispanic Professional Engineers (SHPE), MAES: Latinos in Science and Engineering, and Hispanic Engineer National Achievement Awards Corporation. These particular groups help connect DoD with Hispanics who have science, technology, engineering, and math (STEM) qualifications for many mission-critical DoD occupations. Partnerships with these organizations can involve participation in events that they sponsor, giving DoD access to potential Hispanic applicants.

Other outreach strategies that interviewees mentioned included engaging alumni in college recruiting and having Hispanic DoD employees recruit at their alma maters, as well as including photos of Hispanic employees and Spanish-language translations of DoD recruiting materials. Interviewees also suggested that the department work to raise awareness of DoD civilian opportunities with younger Hispanics beginning at the middle school level.

Hiring

We also asked interviewees about hiring strategies that DoD organizations are or could be using to attract Hispanic employees. Interviewees varied in their level of engagement with Hispanic hiring strategies. Many stated that they do not have strategies aimed at hiring Hispanics and emphasized that all applicants had to apply through the USAJOBS process. A few noted that their organizations focus on hiring Hispanics into STEM jobs or mission-critical occupations (MCOs) and building a pipeline of Hispanic employees in these areas but did not offer related strategies used to do so.

Many interviewees mentioned that potential applicants perceive the USAJOBS application process to be cumbersome and that applying requires a long processing time. Some felt that this deters candidates from applying for available positions. Those who do apply might lose patience with the system because they do not receive any feedback for several months. Interviewees noted that it is difficult for DoD to compete with the private sector because of this complex and prolonged application process. For example, private-sector companies can often extend on-the-spot job offers at career fairs or other recruiting events, while DoD recruiters can only direct potential candidates who express interest to USAJOBS.[2] Interviewees expressed frustration with these limitations and noted that university students and other young potential candidates tend to have less patience for this drawn-out and sometimes convoluted process.

Although issues with the USAJOBS process are likely not unique to Hispanic recruiting, they are certainly a consideration when identifying strategies to improve

---

[2]   We include discussion of internship opportunities in Chapter Seven.

the number of Hispanics hired into the department. A few interviewees pointed out that an expedited authority for hiring Hispanics would be very helpful. DoD can use the Schedule A hiring authority (5 CFR § 213.3102) to hire applicants with specified disabilities through a noncompetitive process. Our interviewees expressed interest in having a similar ability for Hispanic candidates. However, establishing an expedited hiring authority is at the discretion of OPM and would likely not be legal for a demographic group, such as Hispanics.

Promotion and Retention

We also asked DoD interviewees about strategies used to support promotion and retention of Hispanic DoD employees. They identified few efforts. Some noted that their organizations did not have any efforts targeted at promoting and retaining Hispanics. Most interviewees mentioned mentoring programs as a potential promotion and retention strategy. These programs were mostly intended for all employees rather than aimed at specific groups, such as supporting Hispanic employees. A small number of interviewees noted efforts to connect Hispanic mentors with Hispanic mentees within these broader formal programs.

Another strategy that roughly a quarter of interviewees mentioned is employee resource groups (ERGs).[3] Interviewees noted that ERGs for Hispanic employees can be used to communicate career-development opportunities to group members and improve the promotion potential of these employees. Hispanic ERGs can also support Hispanic employees and help build community within organizations, resulting in increased retention.

Promising Department of Defense Practices

We outline two promising DoD practices that a few interviewees mentioned for addressing potential barriers to Hispanic representation.

Hispanic Engagement Action Team Initiative

One promising practice that interviewees noted to improve Hispanic representation is the U.S. Navy Naval Air Systems Command's (NAVAIR's) Hispanic Engagement Action Team (HEAT) initiative. HEAT was founded in 2009 and seeks to build a diverse workforce with increased Hispanic representation. It focuses on recruiting, retaining, and developing Hispanic employees in addition to identifying potential barriers to increased Hispanic representation. HEAT aims to promote a welcoming and inclusive work environment for Hispanic employees.

HEAT members are volunteers, and SES sponsors the HEAT program. Subteams within HEAT tackle specific potential barrier areas, such as recruitment and retention. This structure is replicated across NAVAIR, with each site having a HEAT site

---

[3] ERGs are employee-run groups in which employees (typically with shared identities or experiences) voluntarily form a network within an organization. ERGs associated with demographic groups are common in organizations.

lead and subteams. HEAT efforts are site-based to target challenges unique to each NAVAIR site. Strategies are shared at a national level to maximize effectiveness and lessons learned.

HEAT is taking proactive action to address challenges at each site and increase overall Hispanic representation in NAVAIR. Although we acknowledge that this is a promising practice within DoD, we do not have data to confirm HEAT's effectiveness.

Student Training and Academic Recruitment Program

RAD manages the Student Training and Academic Recruitment (STAR) program, which hires students part time as on-campus representatives and advocates for DoD civilian career opportunities (DCPAS, undated [b]). STAR representatives market DoD careers to fellow students by hosting information sessions, participating in career fairs, and other peer-to-peer interactions.

The first STAR students joined the program in 2007. Four universities—Michigan Technological University; University of Puerto Rico, an HSI; Tennessee State University, a historically black college or university (HBCU); and Rochester Institute of Technology, which houses the National Technical Institute for the Deaf—each with a STAR student, now participate in the program. The STAR program aims to raise awareness about DoD civilian opportunities in student populations that are diverse, as well as those that are somewhat remote and have limited exposure to DoD opportunities. RAD also ensures that universities selected to participate in the STAR program have students with skills that align with DoD civilian job demands. As an HSI representative, the University of Puerto Rico's STAR representative has access to a large pool of qualified Hispanic students, helping the program leverage outreach to Hispanics regarding DoD opportunities.

STAR representatives receive one week of on-site training and orientation in the District of Columbia area. After orientation, STAR representatives work off site at their universities but are in regular contact with RAD personnel. STAR representatives also engage with DoD's Recruiters' Consortium about specific internship or job opportunities available to students across the department. STAR representatives walk fellow students through the USAJOBS process to help facilitate the application process.

Although data are not available to assess whether the STAR program has increased the number and diversity of DoD applicants or hires, RAD personnel report that the program is highly effective in raising awareness of DoD civilian opportunities.

Summary

Our interviews with DoD representatives found that structural and perceptions of behavioral and psychological barriers might contribute to Hispanic underrepresentation in DoD. The most–frequently mentioned potential barriers included the geographic location of DoD positions, perceptions of language or citizenship barriers, and a lack of awareness and motivation from leaders and managers to address Hispanic underrepresentation.

Although interviewees reported varying levels of effort related to Hispanic outreach in their organizations, as well as a lack of strategies specifically targeted at Hispanics, they also noted strategies that could be used to a greater extent. These included partnerships with professional Hispanic groups and recruitment at HSIs and in geographic areas with high Hispanic populations.

Interviewees noted challenges with the USAJOBS process and perceived the process as cumbersome and time-consuming. They said that Hispanic applicants could be deterred from applying or could lose patience with the system, making it difficult for DoD to compete with the private sector for Hispanic applicants. Although interviewees stated that few strategies exist to promote and retain Hispanic employees, many noted mentoring programs and Hispanic ERGs as helpful for communicating career-development opportunities and building a community for Hispanic employees. Interviewees also said that NAVAIR's HEAT initiative and the DoD STAR program offered promise for increasing Hispanic representation. We review recommendations regarding these and other programs in Chapter Eight.

CHAPTER SEVEN

Qualitative Assessment of Hispanic Representation Gaps in the Department of Defense Civilian Workforce: Engaging Hispanic-Serving Institutions

To complement our interviews with DoD personnel, we also interviewed representatives of HSIs about how public and private organizations engage with students at universities with large Hispanic populations regarding employment opportunities. In this chapter, we summarize our findings.

Overview of Qualitative Analysis and Methodology

To identify appropriate HSI representatives to interview, we sought guidance from the Hispanic Association of Colleges and Universities (HACU). HACU, a national education association representing HSIs—that is, colleges and universities with at least 25 percent Hispanic enrollment—provided relevant contacts at HSI career centers across the country. We interviewed representatives from California State University, Los Angeles; California State University, San Bernardino; Colorado State University–Pueblo; Florida International University; New Jersey City University; University of New Mexico; University of Texas at El Paso; and University of Texas at San Antonio, as well as from two community colleges that are HSIs, Palo Alto College and Valencia College.

In addition to HSI representatives, we interviewed representatives of non-DoD federal agencies, including the U.S. Department of State and U.S. Department of Homeland Security, regarding their perspectives on Hispanic employment. We selected these agencies from among those that HSI representatives identified as having promise for increasing Hispanic representation in their workforces.

In all, we conducted 13 semistructured interviews roughly one hour in length with HSI and other non-DoD personnel. We asked HSI representatives about the types of organizations recruiting at their universities; outreach, recruitment, hiring, and retention strategies these organizations employ or should employ to be most effective; and reasons for Hispanic underrepresentation in some organizations. See online Appendix G for the full interview protocol. We coded the content of our interview notes and analyzed them to identify key themes and trends. We also reviewed any supporting documents that participants provided.

Qualitative Assessment Findings

In this section, we describe our findings from our HACU interview, then findings from our interviews with HSI representatives, and finally from an interview with a representative of a federal agency that HSI representatives cited as having promising practices.

The Hispanic Association of Colleges and Universities

We first spoke with HACU to identify relevant universities to speak with and to learn more about HACU's programs partnering with HSIs and promoting employment opportunities for students. HACU helped us identify HSIs that were highly involved in HACU's activities and would be best positioned to provide useful perspectives on effective recruitment strategies of their student bodies. HACU represents more than 470 colleges and universities committed to the higher education of Hispanics and that, collectively, represent more than two-thirds of all Hispanic college students nationwide. HACU's work aims to champion successful higher education of Hispanics.

Although HACU does not recruit at HSIs on behalf of employers for full-time permanent employment, its efforts include the HACU National Internship Program (HNIP), which connects students from HSIs to internships at federal government agencies and private employers. For many federal agencies, the HNIP is used as a strategy to build a pipeline of Hispanic candidates for permanent employment after graduation. Our HACU interviewee noted that, currently, DoD provides very limited internship opportunities through this program. In 2014, DoD accounted for just nine of 386 HNIP interns at federal agencies.[1] According to HACU, additional DoD opportunities in the HNIP would allow DoD to increase engagement with students from HSIs. Interviews with HSI representatives present additional strategies to more effectively engage with Hispanic students.

Effective Practices That Organizations at Hispanic-Serving Institutions Use

HSI representatives identified several strategies that they found to be effective for organizations seeking to engage with their students about potential employment. Although we asked HSIs about potential strategies to retain their students once employed, their perspectives, not surprisingly, focused on strategies regarding outreach, recruiting, and the hiring process.

HSI representatives emphasized that agencies need to brand their organizations. Organizations should actively market to students so that they understand what the organization has to offer and what makes its employment opportunities interesting. This marketing should be cognizant of the demographic targeted, such as using social

---

[1]   The nine 2014 DoD HNIP interns participated in internships with DLA, Naval Supply Systems Command, and Naval Sea Systems Command Naval Surface Warfare Center Carderock Division.

media to be more appealing to youths. As part of branding and connecting with students more effectively, HSI representatives reported that organizations also need to have an ongoing visible presence on campuses. This means going beyond attendance at annual job fairs. It might include engaging with students through hosting organization information sessions and connecting with relevant faculty and university departments to make presentations in classes.

HSI representatives also suggested connecting with relevant student organizations. These could include student groups in academic majors that align with organizational needs, such as engineering student groups, to meet organizational STEM needs. National-level Hispanic organizations, such as SHPE, often have local student chapters at HSIs that organizations could target for campus outreach, inform them of their employment opportunities, and look for opportunities to engage with students through information sessions or informal networking sessions.

Like some DoD interviewees, HSI representatives also emphasized the importance of Hispanic alumni involvement in recruiting. Representatives felt that students are more likely to connect with recruiters if they have once been in a similar situation. Students might be more willing to consider a move to a different area of the country or work for an organization they had not previously considered if they connect with someone from a similar background who has made those career decisions successfully.

HSI representatives stressed the importance of engaging with students early in their college careers. They said that organizations should not focus their outreach efforts only on university seniors who are actively job seeking, but rather that organizations will have more success if they raise awareness of opportunities in students' freshman or sophomore years. This engagement can include connecting with student organizations from freshmen to seniors and by engaging in or hosting events that encourage attendance from freshmen and sophomores, as well as juniors and seniors.

HSI representatives suggested internships as another effective way to engage students earlier in their college careers. They noted that internships were an effective way for students to try out an organization with limited commitment, as well as for organizations to employ a student on a trial basis. Students who complete internships might be not only more likely to apply for full-time employment but also to share their experiences with other students, further raising awareness of organizations with internships.

Department of Defense–Specific Challenges and Strategies

HSI representatives reported that DoD tended to have limited participation in the effective engagement strategies identified above. Beyond increasing use of these strategies, we asked interviewees for their perspectives on DoD-specific challenges to increasing Hispanic students' interest in DoD employment opportunities and additional strategies DoD should consider.

Consistently with our findings from interviewees with DoD personnel, HSI representatives noted that students perceive the USAJOBS process as complex and time-consuming. They believed that the complexity of this process deters some students from applying. They also claimed that students who do apply often are discouraged by the length of time the process takes to provide them with feedback, in contrast to the quick turnaround of job offers from the private sector. OPM often holds workshops for students on navigating the USAJOBS process, but HSI representatives suggested that DoD ensure that those workshops are occurring at HSIs and consider supplementing them either in person or through webinars.

HSI representatives also suggested that DoD personnel follow up with promising potential applicants after recruiting events to encourage them to apply and answer questions about the USAJOBS process. This follow-up could continue throughout the application process to reassure promising applicants that their applications were being considered and to encourage them to wait for potential DoD job offers before accepting opportunities with other organizations. HSI representatives said that it could be very discouraging for students to apply through USAJOBS and not hear any feedback for several months.

HSI representatives said that students were often unaware of DoD civilian careers and associate DoD opportunities strictly with uniformed military service. Interviewees noted that, although there is sometimes a visible military presence on campus, rarely is there a DoD civilian presence. They suggested better communicating DoD civilian opportunities and career paths to students to increase awareness and in a manner that is interesting and appealing for youths, perhaps by profiling the career paths of several particularly exciting DoD civilian jobs.

As DoD representatives noted, HSI interviewees said that Hispanic students might hesitate to move to a new area of the country where DoD opportunities might be located. Interviewees proposed that DoD try connecting with students' families to explain job opportunities and what DoD has to offer. These efforts can include offering overview materials about DoD opportunities in English and Spanish to provide families with better understanding of DoD civilian careers. DoD can also invite students' families to information sessions on campus to learn more and ask questions to put them more at ease. HSI representatives noted that, by making students' families feel more comfortable about job opportunities and moves, students are often more willing to accept a position outside their current locations or hometowns. Additionally, DoD can work to build networks for new Hispanic employees once they have relocated to ease the transition to a new area.

Considerations for Engagement with Community Colleges

Community-college students represent potential talent pools for employers, including DoD. Hispanic students form a large proportion of community-college populations. Interviews with community-college representatives suggest that, to effectively engage with these students, DoD should consider better tailoring outreach and recruitment efforts.

Representatives emphasized a lack of understanding of DoD civilian opportunities among community-college students. Not only are students often not aware of civilian opportunities in DoD; they do not know what education and experience are required for these positions. Our interviewees noted that DoD outreach to community-college students would help increase awareness about DoD civilian careers and application requirements. In particular, clearly outlined DoD civilian career paths, salaries, and other benefits might pique students' interest.

Community-college students often balance their education with other obligations, such as work and providing for family. These students might have less time on campus than those at four-year universities. Our interviewees said that company information sessions held when students are not normally on campus might get low turnout. They suggested instead that organizations engage students through relevant faculty and academic departments. For example, employers can connect with students by serving as guest lecturers or making brief presentations during relevant class lectures. Community-college representatives noted that engagement with faculty is key for employers to have face-to-face interaction with students.

Finally, our interviewees stressed that the influence of family can be even stronger for Hispanic community-college students than it is for other Hispanic students. Community-college students often live at home with their families. Hence, engaging students' families is particularly important to encourage such students to consider and possibly relocate for DoD civilian careers.

Promising Practice: The State Department's Diplomat in Residence Program

HSI representatives cited the State Department's Diplomat in Residence (DIR) program as an effective strategy to engage with students. We interviewed a representative from the DIR program to learn more about the program and how the State Department uses the program to increase Hispanic representation in its workforce.

The DIR program is designed to raise awareness about employment opportunities at the State Department and build a pipeline of diverse qualified candidates. The program consists of senior and midlevel foreign service officers serving as DIRs as a domestic tour for a regular one- to two-year rotational assignment. DIRs act as forward-deployed recruiters, each representing a particular U.S. region and based at a university. Nationally, there are 16 DIRs in the program. Seven DIRs are based at HSIs or HBCUs, demonstrating the diversity focus of this program. The program continually evaluates which universities should serve as hosts for DIRs to ensure that the host universities selected are aligned with the State Department's targeted recruiting efforts.

DIRs engage with university students in a variety of ways, including connecting with student organizations, working with university career centers, providing information sessions on the State Department application process, and serving as guest lecturers in university departments aligned with their subject-matter expertise. They engage in these activities at their host universities and travel to other universities in their regions. DIRs seek not only to raise general awareness about careers at the State Department but also to provide information about internship opportunities at the undergraduate and graduate levels. At universities that are not HSIs or HBCUs, DIRs still seek to make an impact on diversity by connecting with relevant student groups, such as black fraternities and sororities.

In addition to engaging at universities, DIRs reach out to local communities in their regions. They aim to increase awareness of the State Department at an earlier age and engage with high school students in the area. The State Department is a very competitive organization, offering employment to only roughly 3 percent of applicants. For applicants to be competitive, they must begin to prepare for State Department careers at an early age—hence the need for early engagement from the DIR program. DIRs also reach out to relevant professional organizations in the local communities, in particular those with membership of racial and ethnic minorities.

Our State Department interviewee said that the resources required for the DIR program are considered minimal. Foreign service officers would receive State Department salaries regardless. The interviewee did note that there is a value cost for the DIRs' salaries because they could be using this time in a different assignment. The DIR program has recently included midlevel officers as DIRs, rather than having exclusively senior officers. This has helped reduce the salary-to-value cost. Because DIRs are based at universities, there are no overhead costs for office facilities beyond a Blackberry and laptop and no administrative-support costs. Program costs do include travel and recruiting-event participation costs. There are also roughly ten recruiters in the District of Columbia area who are part of the DIR program and participate in mostly national-level recruiting events. In total, the State Department interviewee reported, the program costs roughly $500,000 annually.

The DIR program representative we interviewed said that the program makes an impact on outreach and recruiting by being on the ground, out in the field. Although that sounds promising, quantifying the program's effect on the diversity of the State Department's workforce is difficult. The average age of a State Department hire is early 30s because, the interviewee noted, it takes that amount of time for someone to gain the education and experience to be a competitive applicant. Although someone might have interacted with a DIR as a student, it might be many years from the time that person speaks with a DIR to the time the candidate applies for a position at the State Department.

The DIR program is beginning to collect data to understand the program's impact, but this has been very recent, and often only anecdotal data are available. Newly sworn officers are now asked why they joined the State Department and whether they interacted with DIRs. Nevertheless, given the many contributors to a State Department career, isolating the DIR program's impact remains difficult.

Summary

HSI representatives noted several strategies that organizations use to effectively connect with students regarding employment opportunities. These included organizations branding themselves by actively marketing their opportunities to students, as well as having a visible presence on campus beyond attending job fairs or similar events. Interviewees also mentioned that connecting with relevant student organizations on campus and involving alumni in recruiting efforts are effective strategies. They stressed that early engagement was important and that organizations should focus on outreach to students earlier in their college careers, potentially through promoting internship opportunities.

HSI representatives also noted that DoD had limited engagement in the effective strategies outlined above and identified challenges and potential solutions specific to DoD. Consistently with challenges that DoD interviewees mentioned, HSI representatives stated that students find the USAJOBS process complex and time-consuming. They recommended that DoD follow up with promising applicants throughout the application process to keep them engaged. Interviewees also noted a lack of awareness of DoD civilian opportunities among students and suggested that DoD communicate job opportunities and career paths in ways interesting and appealing to youths to increase awareness and interest. HSI representatives said that students might hesitate to relocate to new areas of the country and suggested that DoD connect with students' families when possible, as well as work to build networks for new employees once relocated. Interviewees also identified the State Department DIR program as a promising practice to engage with students regarding employment opportunities and increase awareness about careers in government. We present recommendations based on these findings in Chapter Eight.

Conclusion and Recommendations

Our assessments of DoD internal and external trends in Hispanic representation, analyses of the extent to which DoD workforce characteristics can influence Hispanic representation, examination of DoD applicant and application characteristics, and consideration of DoD and HSI representative perspectives suggest several potential avenues that DoD can pursue to continue to assess and improve Hispanic representation in the DoD civilian workforce. In this chapter, we offer several recommendations to guide these efforts.

Expand Department of Defense Outreach to the Hispanic Population, Especially to Younger Hispanic Workers in U.S. Hispanic Population Centers

The DoD workforce is representative of the CLF only after structural aspects of DoD (e.g., age, education, location) are taken into account. This implies that the Hispanic representation gap in DoD will not improve without proactive efforts to increase the Hispanic awareness of work for DoD, relative to other demographic groups.

One way to mitigate the Hispanic representation gap is for DoD, including ODMEO and individual agencies within DoD, to expand outreach efforts aimed at the Hispanic population. In expanding outreach, DoD can employ well-informed, targeted efforts. It should leverage practices from other federal agencies because non-DoD agencies appear to outperform DoD despite having similar limitations (such as citizenship requirements). DoD efforts should especially focus on younger potential employees because DoD underrepresentation of Hispanic employees is worse among younger personnel. Because the advertised location of a job appears to affect Hispanic applicants, the large DoD presence in a few highly Hispanic states is a natural advantage. However, the analysis of job-applicant locations suggests that more opportunities exist in highly Hispanic areas without large DoD footprints. By increasing outreach to new areas, DoD could increase visibility among a greater number of diverse and qualified applicants. Notably, DoD will need to consider the availability and adequacy of relocation allowances, such that workers might be more likely to relocate for positions that have relocation allowances.

These analyses provide some information on application patterns of Hispanic workers but cannot identify the underlying behavioral mechanisms behind those patterns. For example, the fact that few Hispanic applicants from Texas originated outside San Antonio could mean that Hispanic workers in other areas were unaware of DoD opportunities, or it could mean that the workers are unwilling to move for such opportunities. DoD could perform market research to identify the aspects of DoD employment that most appeal to Hispanic civilian workers. Such research could allow more-effective recruiting and illuminate why younger Hispanic workers are less likely to work for DoD and, relatedly, why Hispanic workers are less likely to apply for recent-graduate or intern positions in DoD. This research can also elucidate which location and job elements most appeal to the population of interest, which can assist with marketing efforts, and what will encourage younger workers to move to new locations.

Increase Department of Defense Presence with Hispanic Student Populations at Colleges and Universities, Particularly Hispanic-Serving Institutions

In addition to expanding outreach to large Hispanic population centers, DoD should seek to increase its presence among Hispanic students at colleges and universities, particularly HSIs. ODMEO and individual DoD agencies, including the services, can support and conduct such outreach efforts. This will increase awareness not only of DoD civilian opportunities but also of the DoD application process and allow face-to-face interactions with potential applicants. Through these increased on-campus efforts, DoD can connect with families of Hispanic students to inform them of what DoD careers can offer to graduates and assuage reservations about potential moves to new areas of the country. Where possible, DoD should also involve DoD employees who are HSI alumni in campus recruiting efforts at their alma maters.

To institutionalize an on-campus presence, DoD should consider the feasibility of instituting a program at HSIs that would be similar to the State Department's DIR program. DoD employees would reside at HSIs on a rotation to actively engage and recruit students and members of the local community.[1] DoD could consider selecting participants for the rotation in occupations in which DoD seeks to build a pipeline of

---

[1]   Notably, the DIR and STAR programs are promising practices, but, if they are implemented or expanded, DoD needs to invest resources in an evaluation, which would permit assessment of impact.

Hispanics, such as in STEM fields. The costs for such a program, including its implementation, appear to be relatively small.[2]

DoD can further leverage existing programs to expand their reach and impact on Hispanic representation. DoD should expand its STAR program as a tool for diversity recruiting by targeting a broader base of HSIs beyond the University of Puerto Rico, currently the only HSI participating in the program. Not only would this provide an opportunity to hire a Hispanic student as the STAR representative who might opt to apply for full-time DoD employment at graduation; it would also offer DoD access to the STAR student's peers. DoD could consider selecting STAR representatives at HSIs in STEM fields or other academic areas in which it wishes to build a strong pipeline of Hispanic applicants aligned with MCOs. By expanding the STAR program at HSIs, DoD could increase awareness of DoD civilian careers among Hispanic students. Although, at this time, funding limitations restrict STAR program expansion, perhaps there will be opportunities in the future to do so.[3]

One way DoD can increase engagement with Hispanic students that does not require on-campus presence is through HACU's internship program. Currently, DoD has limited engagement with the HACU internship program. However, when DoD components have internship opportunities available, they can provide this information to the HACU program and work with HACU to fill these internships with students from HSIs. HACU works to market the program's internship opportunities and provide participating organizations with qualified HSI student candidates. DoD should increase its participation in the HACU internship program not only to raise awareness about DoD within HSI student communities but also to build a pipeline of students who might pursue full-time employment with DoD after graduation.

Finally, DoD should participate in additional outreach efforts beyond HSIs. For instance, DoD should increase engagement with professional Hispanic organizations, such as SHPE, to leverage beneficial partnerships to improve Hispanic recruiting. DoD is already engaging in partnerships with professional Hispanic organizations to some degree, but it can expand these efforts and ensure that partnerships are fully leveraged. DoD's outreach efforts beyond those with HSIs should also engage high schools and communities with high Hispanic representation. Raising awareness earlier in youths and with families of students is key to successful outreach in the Hispanic community.

---

[2] We recognize that the Intergovernmental Personnel Act (IPA) (Pub. L. 91-648, 1971) Mobility Program enables DoD and other federal government employees to participate in temporary assignments at colleges and universities in addition to other organizations. The IPA program, however, does not have a recruitment focus, and its goals do not parallel those of the State Department's DIR program. A DIR-like program for DoD would be distinct from existing IPA opportunities.

[3] The Partnership for Public Service has a similar program of federal student ambassadors in which DoD could also consider participating (Partnership for Public Service, undated).

Stay Engaged with Promising Candidates During the Application Process, and, When Possible, Leverage Appropriate Hiring Authorities

DoD can also address potential barriers to increased Hispanic representation among its job candidates. Our findings identified the USAJOBS process as a potential barrier because it was reported as being perceived as complex and taking a great deal of time to receive feedback regarding potential job offers. This complexity and lack of timely feedback could lead qualified applicants of any race or ethnicity to assume that their applications are not under consideration and discontinue the DoD application process. To combat this potential barrier, DoD should encourage recruiters, hiring managers, and other relevant personnel to follow up with promising candidates during the process to encourage them to stay engaged with DoD and deter them from accepting employment elsewhere while waiting for DoD job offers. These follow-ups should be performed by the office advertising a job position and could include updates regarding the application review timeline, including when the office expects to conduct interviews and make a decision regarding the position, and could encourage applicants to send additional questions.

Although some interviewees suggested an expedited hiring authority for Hispanics, we do not believe that this is a feasible strategy given the complexity and legal implications of establishing such authority. Instead, we recommend that DoD leverage groups with existing preferences or special hiring authorities that also might have Hispanic representation. For example, this could include further engaging with the military as people separate from the services and connecting with veteran student groups at HSIs with the aim of increasing interest in DoD opportunities from Hispanic veterans who might qualify for veterans' preference for federal government positions. Similarly, DoD can engage HSIs' programs for students with disabilities to encourage applications from Hispanic people with disabilities who might qualify for the Schedule A noncompetitive hiring authority.

Support the Development of Hispanic-Friendly Communities in the Workplace Through Employee Resource Groups and Mentoring

To improve promotion opportunities for Hispanic employees and retain Hispanic employees at greater rates, DoD should support the development of Hispanic-friendly communities in the workplace. By fostering an inclusive environment that is welcoming to Hispanics, ODMEO and individual agencies in DoD, including the services, can help Hispanic workers flourish in their jobs and desire to stay in DoD careers. To promote this work environment, DoD should support the establishment of Hispanic ERGs. To help them be effective and have credibility, DoD should ensure that these ERGs have senior-level support and endorsement. These groups can serve as a critical support network by helping new Hispanic employees who have made significant moves adjust to their new locations, advising members on career-development opportunities, and in additional ways.

Mentoring is another strategy DoD can use to foster an inclusive environment and support Hispanic employee promotion and retention, such that previous research suggests that mentoring can be particularly effective for minorities in the workforce (e.g., Thomas, 2001). DoD should increase the emphasis on mentoring Hispanic employees throughout the department. It could do this by leveraging existing mentoring programs available to all employees. Alternatively, DoD components can connect with Hispanic ERGs to establish mentor–mentee relationships between ERG members. We recognize that some DoD components might already offer ERGs and mentoring to some degree, but we recommend that DoD increase these efforts and ensure that they support Hispanic employees in particular.

Encourage Engagement Action Teams

DoD can encourage components to establish engagement action teams similar to NAVAIR's HEAT initiative. The central objectives of these teams would be to build a workforce with increased Hispanic representation and to foster inclusive work environments that welcome Hispanic employees. With critical senior-leader involvement, these teams send a message that Hispanic representation is a priority. Leadership encouraging volunteer participation and engagement across the component can ensure broad support of the program. These teams could also provide the structure necessary to identify and respond to potential barriers that might be unique to a specific location or division while still sharing lessons learned to increase the efficacy of these efforts. Notably, if these are implemented across DoD, DoD needs to invest resources in an evaluation to assess the impact of program implementation.

Improve the Accessibility, Accuracy, and Utility of Job-Applicant Data

Our analyses demonstrated the potential usefulness of job-applicant data but also characterized some limitations in the way DoD collects and uses applicant data. In theory, the fact that DoD processes nearly all applications through a common online system is an opportunity for policymakers to obtain high-quality information to inform recruiting. In practice, however, the data-collection strategy focuses solely on capturing representation at different steps of the process. This is not as helpful as it could be in developing effective recruiting strategies. The analyses also showed that the limited information available could even lead to erroneous conclusions if the nuances of the data-capture process are not understood. This suggests that analytic errors involving data obtained from the USAJOBS website can occur and might be likely to occur over time or across different data analysts.

DoD should review the process of collecting data from USAJOBS with the goal of improving the accuracy of applicant information. DCPAS could lead this review, which should include an examination of why many applicants do not respond to demographic questions. Given the importance of occupation and education in accounting for gaps, the application process should also collect this information from applicants so that barrier analysis can examine it when it is relevant to representation gaps.

DoD could also explore ways to do more with the other information available in each applicant's USAJOBS profile. For instance, each applicant must input his or her current address when creating a profile. This information could be combined with survey data to identify the most-fruitful areas to target with outreach, as well as to measure the effectiveness of recruiting over time. For example, should some DoD agencies desire to target young Hispanic applicants by appealing to HSIs with a large recruiting push, they would benefit from knowing how many new USAJOBS profiles were created in relevant areas during the increased outreach, as well as the sorts of jobs for which these new applicants applied. Such information could help policymakers measure the effectiveness of their efforts and inform future strategies for other agencies.

Summary

Our analyses suggest several contributors to Hispanic underrepresentation in the DoD civilian workforce. Our recommendations address each phase of the employment cycle, from outreach to retention. By implementing the suggested initiatives, DoD can make progress toward overcoming potential barriers to increased Hispanic representation in the department's civilian workforce.

This report provides research-based recommendations that DoD can implement, but subsequent evaluations are needed to determine the impact of each initiative. For example, to assess the impact of increased outreach, DoD could analyze observed changes in applicants who apply to and applications received by DoD. To examine the effects of increasing its presence at colleges and universities, DoD could periodically collect and analyze relevant information from students and personnel at chosen colleges and universities. In addition, DoD could collect relevant information from new hires to assess their perceptions of USAJOBS and the hiring process, which would permit initial assessment of the effects of continued engagement with applicants. To assist with determining how to further develop Hispanic ERGs, DoD could continue to review and build from existing practices in other departments of the federal government; to evaluate the effects of Hispanic ERGs, DoD could conduct interviews or administer surveys to DoD personnel. Overall, well-planned and carefully executed evaluation efforts can inform the actions DoD takes to address Hispanic representation in its workforce.

Bibliography

American Immigration Council, "Latinos in America: A Demographic Profile," Washington, D.C., April 26, 2012. As of January 16, 2017:
https://www.americanimmigrationcouncil.org/research/latinos-america-demographic-overview

Asch, Beth J., Christopher Buck, Jacob Alex Klerman, Meredith Kleykamp, and David S. Loughran, *Military Enlistment of Hispanic Youth: Obstacles and Opportunities*, Santa Monica, Calif.: RAND Corporation, MG-773-OSD, 2009. As of January 16, 2017:
http://www.rand.org/pubs/monographs/MG773.html

Assistant Secretary of Defense for Force Management and Personnel, "The DoD Civilian Equal Employment Opportunity (EEO) Program," Washington, D.C., Department of Defense Directive 1440.1, May 21, 1987; certified current as of November 21, 2003. As of January 25, 2017:
http://www.dtic.mil/whs/directives/corres/pdf/144001p.pdf

Banks, R. Richard, and Jennifer L. Eberhardt, "Social Psychological Processes and the Legal Bases of Racial Categorization," in Jennifer L. Eberhardt and Susan T. Fiske, eds., *Confronting Racism: The Problem and the Response*, Thousand Oaks, Calif.: Sage Publications, 1998, pp. 54–75.

Betancourt, Hector, and Steven R. López, "The Study of Culture, Ethnicity, and Race in American Psychology," *American Psychologist*, Vol. 48, No. 6, June 1993, pp. 629–637.

Biddle, Dan A., and Scott B. Morris, "Using Lancaster's Mid-P Correction to the Fisher's Exact Test for Adverse Impact Analyses," *Journal of Applied Psychology*, Vol. 96, No. 5, September 2011, pp. 956–965.

Biddle, Richard E., "Disparate Impact Reference Trilogy for Statistics," *Labor Law Journal*, Vol. 46, No. 11, November 1995, pp. 651–660.

Borstelmann, Thomas, *The Cold War and the Color Line: American Race Relations in the Global Arena*, Cambridge, Mass.: Harvard University Press, 2001.

Brown, Anna, and Eileen Patten, *Statistical Portrait of Hispanics in the United States, 2012*, Washington, D.C.: Pew Research Center, April 29, 2014. As of January 31, 2015:
http://www.pewhispanic.org/2014/04/29/statistical-portrait-of-hispanics-in-the-united-states-2012

Campbell, Thomas J., "Regression Analysis in Title VII Cases: Minimum Standards, Comparable Worth, and Other Issues Where Law and Statistics Meet," *Stanford Law Review*, Vol. 36, No. 6, July 1984, pp. 1299–1324.

Carter, James Earl, "Providing for Coordination of Federal Equal Employment Opportunity Programs," Washington, D.C.: White House, Executive Order 12067, June 30, 1978. As of January 16, 2017:
https://www.archives.gov/federal-register/codification/executive-order/12067.html

Carter, Robert T., *The Influence of Race and Racial Identity in Psychotherapy: Toward a Racially Inclusive Model*, New York: Wiley, 1995.

Clinton, William Jefferson, "Educational Excellence for Hispanic Americans," Washington, D.C.: White House, Executive Order 12900, February 22, 1994. As of January 25, 2017: https://www.archives.gov/files/federal-register/executive-orders/pdf/12900.pdf

———, "Hispanic Employment in the Federal Government," Washington, D.C.: White House, Executive Order 13171, October 12, 2000. As of January 16, 2017: https://www.gpo.gov/fdsys/pkg/FR-2000-10-16/pdf/00-26716.pdf

Code of Federal Regulations, Title 5, Administrative Personnel, Chapter I, Subchapter B, Part 213, Excepted Service, Subpart C, Excepted Schedules, Schedule A, Section 213.3102, Entire Executive Civil Service. As of January 25, 2017: http://www.ecfr.gov/cgi-bin/text-idx?rgn=div5&node=5:1.0.1.2.22#se5.1.213_13102

———, Title 5, Administrative Personnel, Subchapter B, Civil Service Regulations, Part 720, Affirmative Employment Programs, Subpart B, Federal Equal Opportunity Recruitment Program. As of January 25, 2017: http://www.ecfr.gov/cgi-bin/ text-idx?SID=df626679158496b82f97ae48b2fc215a&mc=true&node=sp5.2.720.b&rgn=div6

———, Title 5, Administrative Personnel, Subchapter B, Civil Service Regulations, Part 720, Affirmative Employment Programs, Subpart B, Federal Equal Opportunity Recruitment Program, Section 720.202, Definitions. As of January 24, 2017: https://www.gpo.gov/fdsys/search/pagedetails.action?packageId= CFR-1998-title5-vol2&granuleId=CFR-1998-title5-vol2-sec720-202&collectionCode=CFR&browse Path=Title+5%2FChapter%2FSubchapter+B%2FPart+720%2FSubpart+B%2FSection+720.202& collapse=true&fromBrowse=true&bread=true

———, Title 29, Labor, Vol. 4, Subtitle B, Regulations Relating to Labor (Continued), Chapter XIV, Equal Employment Opportunity Commission, Part 1607, Uniform Guidelines on Employee Selection Procedures (1978). As of January 24, 2017: http://www.ecfr.gov/cgi-bin/ text-idx?SID=eae69947942d517e90f7f6fb576b8e81&mc=true&node=pt29.4.1607&rgn=div5

———, Title 29, Labor, Subtitle B, Regulations Relating to Employment (Continued), Chapter XIV, Equal Employment Opportunity Commission, Part 1607, Uniform Guidelines on Employee Selection Procedures (1978), Section 1607.4, Information on Impact. As of January 24, 2017: http://www.ecfr.gov/cgi-bin/ text-idx?SID=64c0ccf69513b5cb706d471de91bfa76&node=pt29.4.1607&rgn=div5#se29.4.1607_14

———, Title 29, Labor, Subtitle B, Regulations Relating to Employment (Continued), Chapter XIV, Equal Employment Opportunity Commission, Part 1607, Uniform Guidelines on Employee Selection Procedures (1978), Section 1607.4, Information on Impact, Paragraph D, Adverse Impact and the "Four-Fifths Rule." As of January 24, 2017: http://www.ecfr.gov/cgi-bin/ text-idx?SID=64c0ccf69513b5cb706d471de91bfa76&node=pt29.4.1607&rgn=div5#se29.4.1607_14

Cohn, D'Vera, *Millions of Americans Changed Their Racial or Ethnic Identity from One Census to the Next*, Washington, D.C.: Pew Research Center, May 5, 2014. As of January 27, 2015: http://www.pewresearch.org/fact-tank/2014/05/05/ millions-of-americans-changed-their-racial-or-ethnic-identity-from-one-census-to-the-next/

Cokley, Kevin, and Germine H. Awad, "Conceptual and Methodological Issues Related to Multicultural Research," in P. Paul Heppner, Bruce E. Wampold, and Dennis M. Kivlighan, eds., *Research Design in Counseling*, 3rd ed., Belmont, Calif.: Thomson Brooks/Cole, 2008, pp. 366–385.

Compton, Elizabeth, Michael Bentley, Sharon Ennis, and Sonya Rastogi, *2010 Census Race and Hispanic Origin Alternative Questionnaire Experiment: Final Report*, Washington, D.C.: U.S. Census Bureau, February 28, 2013. As of January 16, 2017:
https://www.census.gov/2010census/pdf/2010_Census_Race_HO_AQE.pdf

DCPAS—*See* Defense Civilian Personnel Advisory Service.

Defense Civilian Personnel Advisory Service, "RAD Mission," undated (a). As of January 25, 2017:
http://godefense.cpms.osd.mil/about_RADmission.aspx

———, "RAD Programs," undated (b). As of January 25, 2017:
http://godefense.cpms.osd.mil/about_programs.aspx

DoD—*See* U.S. Department of Defense.

DoDD 1020.02—*See* Under Secretary of Defense for Personnel and Readiness, 2009.

DoDD 1440.1—*See* Assistant Secretary of Defense for Force Management and Personnel, 1987 (2003).

Dunleavy, Eric M., "A Consideration of Practical Significance in Adverse Impact Analysis," Washington, D.C.: DCI Consulting Group, July 2010. As of February 1, 2017:
http://dciconsult.com/whitepapers/PracSig.pdf

EEO MD-715—*See* U.S. Equal Employment Opportunity Commission, 2003.

EEOC—*See* U.S. Equal Employment Opportunity Commission.

Ennis, Sharon R., Merarys Ríos-Vargas, and Nora G. Albert, *The Hispanic Population: 2010*, Washington, D.C.: U.S. Census Bureau, May 2011. As of May 12, 2016:
http://www.census.gov/content/dam/Census/library/publications/2011/dec/c2010br-04.pdf

EO 11935—*See* Ford, 1976.

EO 12067—*See* J. Carter, 1978.

EO 12900—*See* Clinton, 1994.

EO 13171—*See* Clinton, 2000.

EO 13562—*See* Obama, 2010.

EO 13583—*See* Obama, 2011.

Federal Hispanic Work Group, *Report on the Hispanic Employment Challenge in the Federal Government*, Washington, D.C.: U.S. Equal Employment Opportunity Commission, October 23, 2008. As of September 21, 2015:
http://www.eeoc.gov/federal/reports/hwg.html

Ford, Gerald, "Citizenship Requirements for Federal Employment," Washington, D.C.: White House, Executive Order 11935, September 2, 1976.

Fry, Richard, and Paul Taylor, *Hispanic High School Graduates Pass Whites in Rate of College Enrollment: High School Drop-Out Rate at Record Low*, Washington, D.C.: Pew Research Center, May 9, 2013. As of January 16, 2017:
http://www.pewhispanic.org/2013/05/09/
hispanic-high-school-graduates-pass-whites-in-rate-of-college-enrollment/

Gold, Michael Evan, "Griggs' Folly: An Essay on the Theory, Problems, and Origin of the Adverse Impact Definition of Employment Discrimination and a Recommendation for Reform," *Industrial Relations Law Journal*, Vol. 7, No. 4, January 1985, pp. 429–598. As of January 16, 2017:
http://digitalcommons.ilr.cornell.edu/cbpubs/9/

Greenberg, Irwin, "An Analysis of the EEOCC 'Four-Fifths' Rule," *Management Science*, Vol. 25, No. 8, August 1979, pp. 762–769.

Griffin, Deborah H., "Measuring Survey Nonresponse by Race and Ethnicity," *Joint Statistical Meetings Proceedings: Section on Survey Research Methods*, Alexandria, Va.: American Statistical Association, 2002, pp. 1254–1259. As of January 16, 2017: http://ww2.amstat.org/sections/SRMS/Proceedings/y2002/Files/JSM2002-000954.pdf

Hemphill, F. Cadelle, Alan Vanneman, and Taslima Rahman, *Achievement Gaps: How Hispanic and White Students in Public Schools Perform in Mathematics and Reading on the National Assessment of Educational Progress*, Washington, D.C.: U.S. Department of Education, National Center for Education Statistics, NCES 2011-459, June 2011. As of January 16, 2017: https://nces.ed.gov/pubsearch/pubsinfo.asp?pubid=2011459

Humes, Karen R., Nicholas A. Jones, and Roberto R. Ramirez, *Overview of Race and Hispanic Origin: 2010*, Washington, D.C.: U.S. Census Bureau, March 2011. As of January 28, 2015: http://www.census.gov/content/dam/Census/library/publications/2011/dec/c2010br-02.pdf

Jacobs, Rick, Paige J. Deckert, and Jay Silva, "Adverse Impact Is Far More Complicated Than the *Uniform Guidelines* Indicate," *Industrial and Organizational Psychology*, Vol. 4, No. 4, December 2011, pp. 558–561.

Kadane, Joseph B., "A Statistical Analysis of Adverse Impact of Employer Decisions," *Journal of the American Statistical Association*, Vol. 85, No. 412, December 1990, pp. 925–933.

Kaye, David H., "Statistical Significance and the Burden of Persuasion," *Law and Contemporary Problems*, Vol. 46, No. 4, Autumn 1983, pp. 13–23.

Kena, Grace, Susan Aud, Frank Johnson, Xiaolei Wang, Jijun Zhang, Amy Rathbun, Sidney Wilkinson-Flicker, and Paul Kristapovich, *The Condition of Education 2014*, Washington, D.C.: U.S. Department of Education, National Center for Education Statistics, NCES 2014-083, May 2014. As of January 16, 2017: https://nces.ed.gov/pubs2014/2014083.pdf

Kenney, Genevieve M., and Douglas A. Wissoker, "An Analysis of the Correlates of Discrimination Facing Young Hispanic Job-Seekers," *American Economic Review*, Vol. 84, No. 3, June 1994, pp. 674–683.

Kochhar, Rakesh, "Latino Jobs Growth Driven by U.S. Born," Washington, D.C.: Pew Research Center, June 19, 2014. As of February 2, 2015: http://www.pewhispanic.org/2014/06/19/latino-jobs-growth-driven-by-u-s-born/

Krogstad, Jens Manuel, and Mark Hugo Lopez, "Hispanic Nativity Shift: U.S. Births Drive Population Growth as Immigration Stalls," Washington, D.C.: Pew Research Center, April 29, 2014. As of January 16, 2017: http://www.pewhispanic.org/2014/04/29/hispanic-nativity-shift/

Lopez, Mark Hugo, "Latinos and Education: Explaining the Attainment Gap," Washington, D.C.: Pew Hispanic Center, October 7, 2009. As of January 16, 2017: http://www.pewhispanic.org/2009/10/07/latinos-and-education-explaining-the-attainment-gap/

Lopez, Mark Hugo, and Jens Manuel Krogstad, "'Mexican,' 'Hispanic,' 'Latin American' Top List of Race Write-Ins on the 2010 Census," Washington, D.C.: Pew Research Center, April 4, 2014. As of January 16, 2017: http://www.pewresearch.org/fact-tank/2014/04/04/mexican-hispanic-and-latin-american-top-list-of-race-write-ins-on-the-2010-census/

McKinley, Scott W., "The Need for Legislative or Judicial Clarity on the Four-Fifths Rule and How Employers in the Sixth Circuit Can Survive the Ambiguity," *Capital University Law Review*, Vol. 37, No. 1, Fall 2008, pp. 171–200.

MD-715—*See* U.S. Equal Employment Opportunity Commission, 2003.

Mead, Alan D., and Scott B. Morris, "About Babies and Bathwater: Retaining Core Principles of the *Uniform Guidelines*," *Industrial and Organizational Psychology*, Vol. 4, No. 4, December 2011, pp. 554–557.

Mitchell, Charles E., "An Analysis of the U.S. Supreme Court's Decision in *Ricci v. DeStefano*: The New Haven Firefighter's Case," *Public Personnel Management*, Vol. 42, No. 1, 2013, pp. 41–54.

Morris, Scott B., and Russell E. Lobsenz, "Significance Tests and Confidence Intervals for the Adverse Impact Ratio," *Personnel Psychology*, Vol. 53, No. 1, March 2000, pp. 89–111.

Mosisa, Abraham T., *Foreign-Born Workers in the U.S. Labor Force*, Washington, D.C.: U.S. Bureau of Labor Statistics, 2013.

Motel, Seth, and Eileen Patten, "The 10 Largest Hispanic Origin Groups: Characteristics, Rankings, and Top Counties," Washington, D.C.: Pew Research Center, June 27, 2012. As of May 12, 2016: http://www.pewhispanic.org/2012/06/27/the-10-largest-hispanic-origin-groups-characteristics-rankings-top-counties/

Neumark, David, "Employers' Discriminatory Behavior and the Estimation of Wage Discrimination," *Journal of Human Resources*, Vol. 23, No. 3, Summer 1988, pp. 279–295.

Nobles, Melissa, *Shades of Citizenship: Race and the Census in Modern Politics*, Stanford, Calif.: Stanford University Press, 2000.

Obama, Barack, "Recruiting and Hiring Students and Recent Graduates," Washington, D.C.: White House, Executive Order 13562, December 27, 2010. As of January 16, 2017: https://www.gpo.gov/fdsys/pkg/FR-2010-12-30/pdf/2010-33169.pdf

———, "Establishing a Coordinated Government-Wide Initiative to Promote Diversity and Inclusion in the Federal Workforce," Washington, D.C., Executive Order 13583, August 18, 2011. As of January 16, 2017: https://www.gpo.gov/fdsys/pkg/FR-2011-08-23/pdf/2011-21704.pdf

Office of Management and Budget, "Standards for the Classification of Federal Data on Race and Ethnicity," *Federal Register*, June 9, 1994.

———, "Standards for the Classification of Federal Data on Race and Ethnicity," *Federal Register*, August 28, 1995.

———, "Revisions to the Standards for the Classification of Federal Data on Race and Ethnicity," *Federal Register*, October 30, 1997a.

———, "Standards for Maintaining, Collecting, and Presenting Federal Data on Race and Ethnicity," Statistical Directive 15, October 30, 1997b.

OMB—*See* Office of Management and Budget.

Omi, Michael, and Howard Winant, *Racial Formation in the United States: From the 1960s to the 1990s*, 2nd ed., New York: Routledge, 1994.

OPM—*See* U.S. Office of Personnel Management.

Partnership for Public Service, "Federal Student Ambassadors," undated. As of January 25, 2017: https://ourpublicservice.org/issues/inspire-and-hire/federal-student-ambassadors.php

Patten, Eileen, "Statistical Portrait of the Foreign-Born Population in the United States, 2010," Washington, D.C.: Pew Research Center, February 21, 2012. As of January 31, 2015:
http://www.pewhispanic.org/2012/02/21/
statistical-portrait-of-the-foreign-born-population-in-the-united-states-2010/

Peresie, Jennifer L., "Toward a Coherent Test for Disparate Impact Discrimination," *Indiana Law Journal*, Vol. 84, No. 3, Summer 2009, pp. 773–802.

Public Law 88-352, Civil Rights Act of 1964, July 2, 1964. As of January 22, 2017:
https://www.gpo.gov/fdsys/pkg/STATUTE-78/pdf/STATUTE-78-Pg241.pdf

Public Law 91-648, Intergovernmental Personnel Act of 1970, January 5, 1971. As of January 25, 2017:
https://www.gpo.gov/fdsys/pkg/STATUTE-84/pdf/STATUTE-84-Pg1909.pdf

Public Law 92-463, Federal Advisory Committee Act, October 6, 1972. As of January 25, 2017:
https://www.gpo.gov/fdsys/pkg/STATUTE-86/pdf/STATUTE-86-Pg770.pdf

Public Law 103-62, Government Performance and Results Act of 1993, August 3, 1993. As of January 25, 2017:
https://www.gpo.gov/fdsys/pkg/STATUTE-107/pdf/STATUTE-107-Pg285.pdf

Roth, Philip L., Philip Bobko, and Fred S. Switzer, "Modeling the Behavior of the 4/5ths Rule for Determining Adverse Impact: Reasons for Caution," *Journal of Applied Psychology*, Vol. 91, No. 3, May 2006, pp. 507–522.

Rushton, J. Philippe, *Race, Evolution, and Behavior: A Life History Perspective*, Port Huron, Mich.: Charles Darwin Research Institute, 2000.

Smedley, Audrey, and Brian D. Smedley, "Race as Biology Is Fiction, Racism as a Social Problem Is Real: Anthropological and Historical Perspectives on the Social Construction of Race," *American Psychologist*, Vol. 60, No. 1, January 2005, pp. 16–26.

Sobol, Marion Gross, and Charles J. Ellard, "Measures of Employment Discrimination: A Statistical Alternative to the Four-Fifths Rule," *Berkeley Journal of Employment and Labor Law*, Vol. 10, No. 3, June 1988, pp. 381–399.

Thomas, David A., "The Truth About Mentoring Minorities: Race Matters," *Harvard Business Review*, Vol. 79, No. 4, April 2001, pp. 98–107.

Toossi, Mitra, "Labor Force Projections to 2022: The Labor Force Participation Rate Continues to Fall," *Monthly Labor Review*, December 2013. As of February 1, 2015:
http://www.bls.gov/opub/mlr/2013/article/
labor-force-projections-to-2022-the-labor-force-participation-rate-continues-to-fall.htm

Under Secretary of Defense for Personnel and Readiness, "Diversity Management and Equal Opportunity (EO) in the Department of Defense," Washington, D.C., Department of Defense Directive 1020.02, February 5, 2009.

USAJOBS, "Help Center," Washington, D.C., undated. Referenced February 9, 2015. As of January 16, 2017:
https://help.USAJOBS.gov/index.php/About_Us

U.S. Bureau of Labor Statistics, *Labor Force Characteristics by Race and Ethnicity, 2013*, Washington, D.C., report 1050, August 2014a. As of February 1, 2015:
http://www.bls.gov/opub/reports/cps/race_ethnicity_2013.pdf

———, "National Hispanic Heritage Month," Washington, D.C., October 1, 2014b. As of February 1, 2015:
http://www.bls.gov/opub/ted/2014/ted_20141001.htm

————, "Labor Force Characteristics of Foreign-Born Workers Summary," Washington, D.C., news release, USDL-16-0989, May 19, 2016. As of February 1, 2015:
http://www.bls.gov/news.release/forbrn.nr0.htm

U.S. Bureau of Labor Statistics and U.S. Census Bureau, *Current Population Survey: Design and Methodology*, Technical Paper 63RV, March 2002. As of January 16, 2017:
https://www.census.gov/prod/2002pubs/tp63rv.pdf

U.S. Census Bureau, Form D-61, U.S. Census 2010, Washington, D.C., January 15, 2009. As of January 28, 2015:
http://www.census.gov/2010census/pdf/2010_Questionnaire_Info.pdf

————, *American Community Survey, Puerto Rico Community Survey: 2010 Subject Definitions*, Washington, D.C., c. 2010. As of January 16, 2017:
http://www2.census.gov/programs-surveys/acs/tech_docs/subject_definitions/
2010_ACSSubjectDefinitions.pdf

————, "2014 National Population Projections," Washington, D.C., last revised March 4, 2015. As of January 31, 2015:
http://www.census.gov/population/projections/data/national/2014.html

U.S. Code, Title 5, Government Organization and Employees, Part III, Employees, Subpart A, General Provisions, Chapter 23, Merit System Principles, Section 2301, Merit System Principles. As of January 16, 2017:
https://www.gpo.gov/fdsys/granule/USCODE-2011-title5/
USCODE-2011-title5-partIII-subpartA-chap23-sec2301

————, Title 5, Government Organization and Employees, Part III, Employees, Subpart F, Labor-Management and Employee Relations, Chapter 72, Antidiscrimination; Right to Petition Congress, Subchapter I, Antidiscrimination in Employment, Section 7201, Antidiscrimination Policy; Minority Recruitment Program. As of January 25, 2017:
https://www.gpo.gov/fdsys/search/pagedetails.action?browsePath=Title+5%2FPart+III%
2FSubpart+F%2FChapter+72%2FSubchapter+I%2FSec.+7201&granuleId=
USCODE-2009-title5-partIII-subpartF-chap72-subchapI-sec7201&packageId=
USCODE-2009-title5&collapse=true&fromBrowse=true&collectionCode=USCODE

U.S. Congress Joint Economic Committee, *America's Hispanic Population: An Economic Snapshot*, Washington, D.C., October 2013. As of February 1, 2015:
http://www.jec.senate.gov/public/?a=Files.Serve&File_id=7a08df2f-2485-422d-806e-0c239bebab5a

U.S. Department of Defense, "Text of the DoD Human Goals Charter," July 29, 1998. As of January 25, 2017:
http://archive.defense.gov/news/newsarticle.aspx?id=43191

————, *Department of Defense Diversity and Inclusion Strategic Plan 2012–2017*, Washington, D.C., April 19, 2012. As of January 26, 2017:
http://diversity.defense.gov/Portals/51/Documents/
DoD_Diversity_Strategic_Plan_%20final_as%20of%2019%20Apr%2012%5B1%5D.pdf

————, *Fiscal Years 2013–2018: Strategic Workforce Plan Report*, Washington, D.C., July 25, 2013. As of January 16, 2017:
http://dcips.dtic.mil/documents/SWPWholeReportCDv2.pdf

————, Office of Diversity Management and Equal Opportunity, *DoD Diversity and Inclusion 2013 Summary Report*, Washington, D.C., c. 2014a. As of January 16, 2017:
http://diversity.defense.gov/Portals/51/Documents/
ODMEO%20Diversity%20and%20Inclusion%20Summary%20Report%20FINAL.pdf

————, "Department of Defense Human Goals," April 28, 2014b. As of January 23, 2017: http://archive.defense.gov/documents/DoD-HumanGoals_4-28-14.pdf

U.S. Department of Energy, *Hispanic Employment Plan*, Washington, D.C., July 1999.

U.S. Equal Employment Opportunity Commission, "List of Workforce Data Tables," Washington, D.C., undated. As of January 28, 2015: http://www.eeoc.gov/federal/directives/715instruct/tables.html

————, "Adoption of Questions and Answers to Clarify and Provide a Common Interpretation of the Uniform Guidelines on Employee Selection Procedures," *Federal Register*, Vol. 44, No. 43, March 2, 1979. As of February 18, 2015: http://www.eeoc.gov/policy/docs/qanda_clarify_procedures.html

————, "Equal Employment Opportunity," Washington, D.C., Equal Employment Opportunity Management Directive 715, October 1, 2003. As of February 9, 2015: http://www1.eeoc.gov//federal/directives/md715.cfm

————, *Instructions to Federal Agencies for EEO MD-715, Section II: Barrier Identification and Elimination*, Washington, D.C., last modified July 20, 2004. As of February 9, 2015: http://www.eeoc.gov/federal/directives/715instruct/section2.html

————, *EEOC Compliance Manual*, Washington, D.C., Equal Employment Opportunity Commission Directive 915.003, July 22, 2008a. As of February 1, 2017: https://www.eeoc.gov/policy/docs/religion.pdf

————, "Facts About Race/Color Discrimination," Washington, D.C., last modified September 8, 2008b. As of January 26, 2015: http://www.eeoc.gov/facts/fs-race.html

————, *Instructions to Federal Agencies for EEO MD-715, Section III: Reporting Requirements and Line-by-Line Instructions*, Washington, D.C., last modified December 12, 2008c. As of January 28, 2015: http://www.eeoc.gov/federal/directives/715instruct/section3.html

————, *Barrier Analysis Training*, Washington, D.C., October 29–30, 2014.

U.S. General Accounting Office, *Equal Employment Opportunity: Hiring, Promotion, and Discipline Processes at DEA*, Washington, D.C., GAO-03-413, June 2003. As of January 16, 2017: http://www.gao.gov/products/GAO-03-413

U.S. Government Accountability Office, *Equal Employment Opportunity: Information on Personnel Actions, Employee Concerns, and Oversight at Six DOE Laboratories*, Washington, D.C., GAO-05-190, February 2005. As of January 16, 2017: http://www.gao.gov/products/GAO-05-190

U.S. Office of Personnel Management, "Data, Analysis and Documentation: Data Policy and Guidance," undated (a). As of January 24, 2017: https://www.opm.gov/policy-data-oversight/data-analysis-documentation/data-policy-guidance/

————, "Diversity and Inclusion: Federal Workforce at a Glance," Washington, D.C., undated (b).

————, "9-Point Plan to Improve the Representation of Hispanics in the Federal Workforce," September 18, 1997a.

————, "OPM Proposes 9-Point Plan to Reverse Hispanic Underrepresentation," news release, September 18, 1997b.

————, *First Annual Report to the President on Hispanic Employment in the Federal Government*, Washington, D.C., October 2001.

———, *Introduction to the Position Classification Standards*, Washington, D.C., August 2009. As of January 16, 2017:
https://www.opm.gov/policy-data-oversight/classification-qualifications/classifying-general-schedule-positions/positionclassificationintro.pdf

———, Office of Diversity and Inclusion, *Government-Wide Diversity and Inclusion Strategic Plan*, Washington, D.C., c. 2011a. As of January 16, 2017:
https://www.opm.gov/policy-data-oversight/diversity-and-inclusion/reports/governmentwidedistrategicplan.pdf

———, *Guidance for Agency-Specific Diversity and Inclusion Strategic Plans*, Washington, D.C., November 2011b. As of January 16, 2017:
https://www.opm.gov/policy-data-oversight/diversity-and-inclusion/reports/diagencyspecificstrategicplanguidance.pdf

———, *Twelfth Annual Report to the President on Hispanic Employment in the Federal Government*, Washington, D.C., September 2013. As of January 16, 2017:
https://www.opm.gov/policy-data-oversight/diversity-and-inclusion/reports/hispanic_sep2013.pdf

———, *Federal Equal Opportunity Recruitment Program (FEORP) Report to Congress: Fiscal Year 2014*, Washington, D.C., February 2016. As of April 22, 2016:
https://www.opm.gov/policy-data-oversight/diversity-and-inclusion/reports/feorp-2014.pdf

Yun, Myeong-Su, "Decomposing Differences in the First Moment," *Economics Letters*, Vol. 82, No. 2, February 2004, pp. 275–280.